"Rod Hairston is a tremendously effective communicator and an inspirational leader. He's had an amazing impact on our football team, our coaching staff, and, really, everybody associated with our program."

John Harbaugh
Head Coach, Baltimore Ravens

"My dad died when I was five years old. That left an empty space that needed to be filled. I'm grateful that I had a role model at every level of football. During my six years with the Baltimore Ravens, Pastor Rod Hairston was that role model for me. He made himself accessible to us players, and he conducted Bible studies in the mornings before practice. He was one of the main reasons for our team's success."

Ben Grubbs
Offensive Lineman, New Orleans Saints

"Pastor Rod Hairston has been a profound spiritual influence on me. He challenged us players to be good husbands and fathers. And he modeled that himself. He talked the talk and walked the walk."

Billy Bajema
Tight End, Baltimore Ravens

"One of the biggest challenges a man will face in life is understanding a woman. Rod Hairston gives powerful and practical insights that will assist any man seeking the tools necessary for meeting the needs of a woman!"

Pastor John K. Jenkins, Sr.
Senior Pastor of First Baptist Church of Glenarden (MD)

"Rod Hairston has written a timely book on a very important subject matter for men. Men will be challenged, encouraged, and equipped to become a courageous coverer who makes a difference in the lives of their wives and daughters."

James "JB" Brown
CBS Sports

TABLE OF CONTENTS

Foreword

Foreword

Men, we are in a battle. And it's not going well.

Our homes, our culture, and even our churches have been invaded. The invaders include promiscuity, divorce, abuse, laziness, and addiction of all kinds. Sadly, problems like these are the direct result of men who neglect or reject the biblical standards for husbands, fathers, and other male role models.

Thank God for a book like Rod Hairston's Cover Her. In a world where too many men settle for less than God's best, Pastor Hairston calls us to do more, to be more.

As Pastor Hairston explains, the concept of covering has deep biblical roots. In the Old Testament, God's people provided safety to travelers passing through their town. They protected the vulnerable from predatory harm. It was a matter of personal responsibility and a matter of obedience to God.

Today, covering is the responsibility of every man, young or old, particularly when it comes to women and children.

Men, we were designed by God to be protectors—physically, emotionally, and spiritually. Everyone in our circle of influence—especially our wives and children—should feel safe in our covering presence.

Each of us is called to assure our families, "I will cover you, no matter what it takes. You can count on me to watch over your physical, emotional, and spiritual well-being. Count on me to provide for your needs. Count on me to nurture your dreams."

As Pastor Hairston notes, our tomorrows will be shaped by how well we cover our loved ones today. We must cover in our homes, our churches, our communities, and beyond. We must usher in what is good—and slam the door right in evil's face.

Cover Her is a clarion call to step up, to man up. This book will help you be the husband that your wife adores. The father a kid can look up to. The man who inspires other men to think, I want to be more like him. Meanwhile, the devil says, "Uh-oh. I am in big trouble with this guy around!"

I urge you to read on and discover what it means to be a man with the courage and the love to cover.

–Dr. Tony Evans, President of The Urban Alternative
& Sr. Pastor of Oak Cliff Bible Fellowship, Dallas Texas

CHAPTER 1
Man-Strength

1

In the Baltimore Ravens locker room, we talk about certain players having man-strength. Some call it "country-strong." Some NFL players, even if they never lifted another weight in their lives, could still dominate on the field. They lift weights because their contracts demand it, not because they need to. They're just unusually, naturally strong. They stand out in a profession where physical strength is a prerequisite for competitive success. If one of these guys were to shake your hand, you might feel like your bones were about to be crushed.

In my many years in the National Football League, I've met lots of guys who were born with man-strength.

As a matter of gender, almost all men are born with some degree of man-strength. We inherited it from Adam, who got it from God. God placed in Adam the natural ability and the attitude necessary to exercise dominion over "every living thing that moves on the earth." (Genesis 1:28) Adam was given strength, which enabled him to produce abundantly from the soil by cultivating and caring for the

Garden of Eden. (Genesis 2:15)   And (before the Fall in Genesis 3) Adam didn't even break a sweat while he worked!

When the animals came along, God gave Adam the authority to name each animal. When Adam gave an animal a name, there was no argument. The Bible says, "That was its name." And each animal's name dictated its behavior. Now that's authority! Adam was making things happen with the man-strength God gave him.

Like Adam, today's man must understand, embrace, and exercise good stewardship over his man-strength. Unfortunately, many of us don't know our own strength. We don't truly understand what we possess. We don't appreciate what strength, direction, caring, and nurturing can accomplish in the lives of others.

For example, we have the power to shape people's destinies with our words, just as Adam shaped his world with his words.

Other men have a different problem. They know they are strong, but they abuse that gift by selfishly taking things from those who are what the Bible calls "weaker vessels." This includes women and children.

Ideally, every man should be taught early in life that he has God-given power—power he must harness for the good of others.

When my son, Jeremy, was 13 and on the edge of puberty, I focused on teaching him about his man-strength. I am so glad I did. Jeremy is 17 now, the only brother to his three sisters. He is quiet, academically brilliant, eloquent, super-athletic, and stop-rush-hour-traffic handsome. (Thank God he looks like his mother!) Most important, he has a committed relationship with Jesus Christ.

However, at 13, Jeremy wasn't interested in much beyond his sports, his video games, and having his own "space." His teenage sisters (two older than Jeremy and one younger) shared the interests of most of their peers: lots of chatter and school-girl drama.

Our drives home from school were filled with the day's "411," with the girls talking over each other, eager to toss in their two cents' worth on the day's happenings. Jeremy, however, sat quietly in the back seat of the family SUV. He wanted nothing to do with the conversation. All he wanted was supper and a nap.

Whenever the girls would ask him how his day was, he'd give them that typical teen-boy look. The look told them, "Why are you asking me these stupid questions? Leave me alone. Don't you know by now—I am *not* interested."

Men and women are different. They communicate differently. In relationships, some of their needs are different. And many of their common needs vary in importance from male to female.

Episodes like this showed me that it was time to teach Jeremy about his man-strength. So I told him, "Son, you're a young man, and your sisters are young ladies. You don't know it right now, but they *like* being around your man-strength. You must understand that your voice, whenever you speak, has an impact on them. Sharp tones and condescending looks tear down your sisters, when all they want is to be in relationship with you. From now on, I expect you to engage them thoughtfully and gently, because your face, your words, and your body language are powerful. Your sisters can feel your displeasure and your disapproval, and they think you don't like them or value them. Show a little care and warmth toward them. Go overboard to be respectful and interested. It'll bless them, and they'll be happy to do anything for you."

I added, "Jeremy, you have man-strength, and you must learn how to use it properly *now*, because someday you're going to be a husband and a father, shaping the lives and destinies of your own wife and kids."

I'm grateful to report that Jeremy "got it." He has taken huge strides when it comes to engaging and nurturing his sisters. And they're loving the new, more-engaging Jeremy! He's become a hero at home. He's learning--far earlier in life than I did--that he was born with power. He is learning how to use that power wisely. He's learning what it means to be a man. These are lessons many of us older men would do well to learn.

What Defines A Man?

Simply put, Western society has lost its direction when it comes to gender definition and identity. Confusion reigns everywhere. The idea of feminized men has been pushed, carted, and craftily escorted onto every stage of American public life: the media, the church, the marketplace, the halls of academia, and even the sports world. We are pressured socially to accept this feminized version of manhood as normal--and even superior to the biblical standard. As the website essence.com put it, "What's God got to do with it?"

Please understand me here— I celebrate the beautiful femininity of my wife, my daughters, and my mom! I am merely speaking against the efforts to erase the things that differentiate male from female.

5

Men and women are different. They communicate differently. In relationships, some of their needs are different, and many of their common needs vary in importance from male to female.

And let's not forget the obvious: Men and women have different physical builds and anatomy. Even from a distance, we can usually distinguish a man from a woman based on physical appearance. Typically, a man's shoulders are more square. We have a distinctive jaw line. And, with some of us, the hair-covered faces are a dead giveaway. A careful observer can also spot differences in the way a man and a woman, stand, sit, and walk.

When God designed men and women, He did so with distinctive differences. A man is, in *part*, defined by the strength of his posture and presentation. He doesn't have to be the stereotypical macho man. But he should have a firm handshake, be able to look another man in the eyes, stand tall, and walk with a sense of male dignity.

Israel's first king, Saul, was distinguished because he stood heads and shoulders above his peers. His successor, King David, was said to be a mighty man of valor, a warrior, and an effective communicator. The Bible also describes him as a handsome guy. Somehow we've dismissed the value of a masculine appearance in today's man. Certainly, appearance isn't everything, but let's admit that it's part of what makes a man a man.

Another thing that defines a man is his God-given authority. Have you ever noticed that men love to solve problems? When a wife tells her husband what a tough day she's endured, whether on the job or in the home, his first response is often . . .

"Did you tell your boss, you're only one person?"

"Did you make the kids take a nap?"

"Did you…?"

"You should have …"

Yes, we love to fix problems and make stubborn circumstances submit to our will.

My wife, Sheri, used to complain that everyone in the house (including Cinders, the dog) obeyed better when I came home. She was baffled by the fact that she could say the same thing to the kids 300 times in the course of a day, with no result. Then I could come in and say it one time and things would just happen. The kids mysteriously figured out what their mom had been trying to get them to do all day long.

Our dog is a great family pet, but sometimes he's a little needy. (Must be something about the Lab/Chow mix.) Everywhere we go in the house, he follows us. That's cool, until company comes over. Then it's a nuisance. As soon as we go from the kitchen to the family room, Cinders tags along, demanding that someone, anyone, rub his head. Sheri has to tell him five times, "Cinders, go." At which point, he plops on the floor three feet away, as if to say, "This is as far as I'm going."

Conversely, I simply snap my fingers and point—and he moves to another room, in the direction of my finger, with his head down and tail between his legs. He can sense where the strongest authority rests.

When God created Adam and Eve, He endowed them both with authority. But the first portion of God-given authority went to the man. God gave him authority to name the animals, authority to cultivate and oversee the garden to maximize its productivity, and even the authority to name Eve.

With authority comes responsibility! It was Adam's job, as the guy with "Level 1" authority, to protect Eve from the words and work of the devil. It was Adam's responsibility to teach the life-saving truth of God to Eve. And it was Adam's job to intervene with authority when the devil began to craftily deceive his wife. Had Adam used his God-given voice of authority, rather than stand silent in the shadows, Eve may not have entertained the deceitful notion that God was withholding His best from her. Had Adam spoken up with authority and resisted Eve's offer to eat the fruit God had forbidden, male authority might be seen as a safeguard to humanity rather than the threat it often is.

Finally, what defines a man is his relationship with responsibility. Before God gave Adam a wife (in Genesis chapter 2), He gave him a job. God put Adam in charge of the garden--"to work it and take care of it." (Genesis 2:15) In essence, God told Adam, "Before I will entrust you with the responsibility of a wife and children, I want to see you hold down a job. I want to see you faithfully cultivate and produce something with the resources I've entrusted to you." At the heart of this directive was this message: "Adam, your responsibility in this space I've assigned to you is to 'worship and obey.'" That's the meaning of "work it and take care of it."

God gave Adam a job, and to do that job well, Adam was to work with his ears and his heart open to his Boss. His attitude and faithfulness to the work were an expression of worship and obedience to God. To be clear, God did not tell Adam to worship his work. He told Adam to worship *Him* by being responsible in his work. The work Adam did in the Garden prepared him to lead and support a family. The Garden was a shaping ground for Adam.

I'll conclude this chapter with a message for my female readers: Ladies, a man who commands respect by his strong presence, is respectful with his God- given authority, and does his job responsibly has the potential to become a great husband. But he must also know how to fulfill his role as a *man*.

Chapter 1 Instant Replay

1. Western society has lost its direction when it comes to gender definition and identity.

2. God did not tell Adam to worship his work. He told Adam to worship *Him* by being responsible in his work. The work Adam did in the Garden prepared him to lead and support a family.

3. A man's authority as a leader brings with it huge responsibility.

CHAPTER 2
The Role of a Man

2

"It's your turn to take out the trash this week."

"I washed the dishes *yesterday*, remember?"

"You should pay the bills. I have too much on my plate."

Household arguments like those above are common to marriage. They might seem like no big deal, but they are rooted in something profound: a man's role in the home, the church, and society.

When a man lives up to his role, life-giving things start to happen. Children are not abused, and they grow up feeling secure and safe. Teen pregnancy rates go down. Drug sales and drug use plummet. Young people avoid jail. Divorces are avoided, and the tragedy of teen suicide loosens its grip on our young people. I firmly believe that every family and societal problem can get better when a man knows how to fulfill his role and takes action.

During the NFL season, teams spend Fridays completing their on-field preparation. They know that the adrenaline-filled, high-stakes physical battle is just two days away. That's why a good Friday practice is vital. However, for NFL players, the most important preparation comes on Saturday morning and evening. And this preparation is more mental than physical. Players and their position coaches gather to review video footage of their opponents and hold the last practice, known as a "walk-thru."

The walk-thru and video reviews have a sole purpose: to ensure players are absolutely clear about their game-day roles—on offense, defense, and special teams. A player who doesn't understand his role is a liability to his teammates. He might even cost his team the game and lose his job on the roster.

In the NFL, mistakes are sometimes called "a blown assignment." A running back fails to block a blitzing linebacker. A safety lets a receiver get behind him.

In life, we men cannot afford to blow our assignments. It's not merely a team that is counting on us; it's all of society.

What are our assignments, our roles as men? I can sum them up in five words.

- Praise

- Protection

- Provision

- Proclamation

- Presentation

Let's look at each role in detail.

Praise

Praise is more than words. Praise is a man's heartfelt response to the God who created him. It's his first and most fundamental role in life--to offer God un-abashed applause for who He is and what He's done. Praise was Adam's first assignment. It was his personal and patriarchal duty to acknowledge sincerely and humbly the lofty and high place of God over all He'd made. God was to be number one in Adam's life. God was more important than his gardening career, his animal enterprise, and even his relationship with the lady in his life. In all he did, Adam was to demonstrate praise and thanksgiving to God.

Even long-time Christians underestimate the importance of praise. But the man who strives to let praise flow from his life to God's throne is poised to fulfill God's destiny for his life. He will achieve this destiny because his life is based on an authentic relationship with his Boss and King.

I understand that vocal and visible expressions of praise are tough for men. Why? Maybe it's a male-pride issue. Or a fear to truly release our emotions.

On the other hand, have you ever seen a bunch of guys cheering on their favorite sports team? Why should football, soccer, basketball, and hockey players get all the praise from us men? Some of us will travel the globe to clap and cheer for our favorite team or athlete.

We jump to our feet. We lift our hands. We shout until we're hoarse—all for mortal men who have done nothing substantial for us. They did not get us our jobs. They didn't heal our sick or injured bodies. And, most likely, they haven't given us wisdom to live by. The truth is, men do understand praise. Our praise is often misdirected.

Our homes and our churches need men who will lead the way when it comes to cheering the mighty works of God. Remember that the role of praise was given to Adam before Eve came along.

> *In too many churches now, the women praise ecstatically, while the men sit uncomfortably, waiting for the worship service to end. And the children take note: "Daddy doesn't like church."*

Adam's role was to keep the praise party going when his wife arrived, so that she would have a model to follow. In too many churches now, the women praise ecstatically, while the men sit uncomfortably, waiting for the worship service to end. And the children take note: "Daddy doesn't like church."

What has happened? In short, the devil has deceived men and convinced us to shut down emotionally in God's presence. But David, a great king and a man's man, danced before the Lord and committed to proclaim His goodness among the people.

Men, if David can do it, we can too. The world is waiting for us to applaud God in the public square, in our homes, and in the house of God. When men offer praise to God, everyone takes note. We are the tone setters in our culture. Like it or not, what we do, everybody does. So, "Let us continually offer the sacrifice of praise to God, that is, the fruit of our lips, giving thanks to His name." (Hebrews 13:15 NKJV)

Protection

When God placed Adam in the Garden of Eden, He told him to "take care of it." God knew that a perpetual and dark threat to His glorious creation was lurking in the shadows. When God established man, a lesser being than the angelic hosts, to give Him unblemished praise, Satan was ready to spread his rebellious wares in the human race. (See Ezekiel 28:11-19 and Isaiah 14:12-21.)

Adam's job was to keep watch and to protect everything entrusted to him from the devil's deception. Adam's role back then is a man's role now. We need to protect our "garden" from the deceptions, dark acts, and destructive works of the devil. Your personal garden is wherever God has assigned you to live, work, and play. The people who inhabit your garden, especially the women and children entrusted to your leadership, are your responsibility to protect.

Don't be like many men in our culture who, like Adam, have shunned the call to protect. Instead, they have become vultures, preying on those who need their strength. Some men have even demanded that the women and children protect them! Something is desperately wrong with this picture.

Bullying in our culture and around the globe is a problem growing with exponential fervor. Typically, kids who bully were unprotected by their own fathers. They act out with resentment toward their peers or toward those who appear weak to them. A society in which men drop the ball of protection is a society of aggression, crime, and hate. But when men use our God-given power to protect, we can turn the tide and bring the sense of safety everybody needs-- the bullies and the bullied.

Provision

Though she was a single mother, my mom was an exceptional provider. We lived in the projects, but she made sure her three sons had everything we needed. That lady still has an amazing work ethic and, my goodness, she can stretch a dollar!

But she was left in a position she was not made for. Divorced at the age of 17 by my alcoholic dad (who also had a gambling habit), she was left on her own to fulfill the role God had given to men- -to be the primary providers for their homes. In his letter to the Thessalonians, Paul didn't say, "If a woman will not work . . . ." He said, "If a man will not work, he will not eat." The role of a man is to do whatever is necessary (legally) to keep food on the table, a leak-free roof over head, clothes on the backs, and shoes on the feet.

I've seen too many men in our culture, especially during the recent economic downturn, curl up in the fetal position and suck on their vocational thumbs. I'm tired of hearing men from church complain, "There aren't any good jobs out there. No one's hiring."

If no one's hiring, create your own job!

I've watched too many men demand that their wives go out and be the primary bread-winner. To me, that's a cop-out. It multiplies stress in already-stressed families and leaves too many children to parent themselves. Too many men are gripped with an unrelenting fear when it comes to being the bread- winner, and I'm convinced that the root cause is spiritual. Satan has struck fear in the hearts of men and blinded us to the power to provide that resides in us.

Some men are like adolescents—addicted to PlayStation 3 and lacking in entrepreneurial courage. They lack the will and discipline to keep the cash flowing into their households.

God gave Adam the best job he ever had, entrusting him with a sprawling estate of lush, fruit-bearing vegetation. He was charged with taking what God created and creatively multiplying it. That is still our task today: to reshape, cultivate, and re-create what God has already made. We work to meet a need, and then charge a reasonable price for the goods or services we render.

The question for every man struggling with his role to provide is the one God asked Moses, "What's in your hand?" What skills, relationships, experiences, education, and passions has God placed in you? Figure it out and use them. God has a job for you. You *can* provide for yourself and your family, but you must be connected to the Job Creator who makes the work fruitful.

Proclamation

A man of few words is usually a wise man. But a man who has nothing to say at critical times is a weak man. It's amazing how, throughout history, God has used a man who was willing to speak up when the times demanded a voice of righteousness and justice. Though Moses was afraid to speak, he said what God told him to say to Pharaoh--and the children of Israel walked on dry land through the sea. Many centuries later, Jesus spoke out against the religious oppression of the Jewish leaders in His community, and Christians around the world now walk into the presence of God through the red blood of Jesus. Dr. Martin Luther King Jr. spoke out against the injustices of racial segregation and the oppression of the poor in America, and now I can live in any neighborhood I choose, eat wherever I can get a dinner reservation, and educate my children on any campus in the nation.

When men speak up rather than being passive, the social, political, spiritual plots of the devil are exposed and defeated. Imagine if Adam had spoken up when the devil tempted Eve in the Garden of Eden. The Bible says, "She also gave [fruit] to her husband with her, and he ate it." (Genesis 3:6 NKJV)

I know I may be in a long line of inquisitors, but I want to ask Adam two questions: "What in the world were you thinking?" and "Why didn't you speak up?"

Adam blew it big-time. He failed to speak up. He should have warned Eve to avoid even a conversation with the serpent, much less letting him tempt her to eat fruit that God had deemed off-limits. Twice in Genesis chapter 2, Adam spoke. The first time was when he named the animals. It was an expression of his God-given authority. The second time was when he was taken with excitement at the gift of his wife. He named her Eve--a second expression of his God-given authority. Having authority from God to speak up is a real privilege. We can only wonder why, at the golden moment of opportunity to defeat Satan, Adam fell eerily silent.

A man's role in society is to speak up when danger is in the environment, to denounce injustice, and to declare with unashamed guts what God has made clear in His Word.

Frankly, we have a generation of Adam look-alikes. They would rather talk about their favorite sports team than the things that truly matter. We have little to say, it seems, about the things devouring our children and our families and our world: the rise of crime, the abuse of women, and worldwide atrocities affecting the poor and downcast. We watch our young daughters prance out of our homes nearly naked and we say nothing. We watch our wives entertain advertised lies about the value of physical beauty and we say nothing. We watch crooked businessmen execute crooked deals, look for our cut, and shut our mouths. We stand by silently as digital pornography invades our homes and the lives of our sons and daughters.

A generation of men who have no truth to proclaim can do nothing to protect and cover our women and children. This leaves a nation (a world!) wide open for the wolves to devour. We must regain our collective courage, open our mouths, and proclaim with authority biblical truth to the criminal and immoral ideologies consuming our culture. We have to man up and speak up.

Presentation

Finally, men have the powerful role and responsibility to *present.* What do I mean by present? We husbands are commanded in Ephesians 5:25-27 to present our wives spotless and blameless. The original statement speaks to the sacrificial love of Jesus toward the church, which He gave His life for.

The Bible says that Jesus will present the church to Himself, pure and blameless. In the same way, husbands are to present to ourselves wives who've been so impacted by our love and by our leadership that they've become beautiful brides to us, just as the church is to Christ! I tell men everywhere I go, "You get out what you put in. If you want a good-looking wife filled with godly character and a heart open to your leadership, you have to pour into her sacrifice, love, and the Word of God. Translation: Spend some money on her and some time with her. Date her. Share with her the wisdom of God that you're learning. And you'll find yourself with an amazing, beautiful woman with a quiet and gentle spirit."

As Billy Bajema, tight end for the world-champion Ravens puts it, "It's time for men to step up and make their families a priority. I want to raise my kids to know and serve the Lord. I want to have a strong marriage that leaves a legacy for our kids."

Like the five points on a star, a man who embraces his five-fold role will shine brightly in the culture and make a significant impact everywhere he goes.

He will provide all-important *covering* for his wife and children.

Chapter 2 Instant Replay

1. I firmly believe that every family and societal problem can get better when a man knows how to fulfill his role and takes action.

2. A generation of men who have no truth to proclaim can do nothing to protect and cover our women and children.

3. If you want a wife filled with godly character and a heart open to your leadership, you have to pour into her sacrifice, love, and the Word of God.

CHAPTER 3
The Call to Cover

3

Watch a televised football game, and you'll hear a lot about covering: "The cornerback blew the coverage." "This quarterback is really good against the Cover 2."

But the subject of covering pre-dates football by thousands of years. The Old Testament talks about covering—in its teaching on hospitality. God commanded the Israelite community to practice warm hospitality toward one another, but also to extend it to neighbors, strangers, and foreigners.

Especially when it came to travel from one community to another, people were vulnerable to the dangers of unfamiliar places. Danger lurked from robbers, thieves, and other assorted unsavory characters. During these days, travelers seeking lodging would make their way to a town square, typically located in the center of a city. Townspeople who observed Jewish law valued hospitality. So they would offer travelers "covering" for the night. This covering was a gesture of God's kindness, grace, and righteousness toward those who would otherwise be exposed to the dangers of the night. In Hebrew culture, it was unthinkable to leave vulnerable people exposed to possible harm, so one would offer the safety of his home, even to a stranger. God was so serious about covering/hospitality that He commanded it of Israel, instructing them to remember that they were once foreigners in a place that was unkind to them: Egypt! (See Deuteronomy 24:17-22.)

So, a man who extends covering is someone who offers safety from predatory harm to the vulnerable who "travel" through his community, his circle of influence. Covering is the responsibility of every man, young and old, particularly when it comes to women and children.

Men, we were designed and assigned by God to be protectors. As we've already seen, when God placed Adam in the Garden, a major part of his job description was to protect it. No one who is weaker than we are–whether physically, emotionally, mentally, or otherwise--should feel unsafe in our presence.

Active Verses Passive Covering

When I teach on the subject of covering at men's conferences and at churches around the country, someone always asks the following questions:

"Are we as men supposed to cover the single women in our church— and how, exactly does that work?"

"I'm a single mom. Am I supposed to come under the covering of the men in my church?"

"Isn't it dangerous for a married man to assume the covering role in the life of a single woman or single mom?"

Wives will ask me, with that suspicious and unsettled look in their eyes, "Are you telling me that my Christian husband is supposed to be covering other women in the church?" They're kind when they ask, but the real translation of their question is, "You must be out of your mind! There's no way in the world I am risking my marriage to have my man 'cover' another woman! I know that's not from God!"

As you can see, the principle of covering can become complicated and convoluted--if we're not careful and if we're not in tune with God's heart. The answer to all the questions above has to do with what's appropriate and honoring to God. God will never endorse anything that jeopardizes the marriage covenant. Nor will He endorse flirtatious and manipulative motives in the hearts of men or women. This brings us to the difference between *active covering* and *passive covering*.

My active covering is the intentional and proactive effort to protect those God has assigned to be under my covering through marriage and birth. (The same would be true of adoption.) With my wife and children, I have a unique and precious relationship. It's a gift from God, and it carries enormous responsibility. I'm called as a husband and a father to assure my family, with pride, purpose, and action: "I will cover you, no matter what it takes. Count on me to provide for your needs. Count on me to look out for your physical, emotional, and spiritual well-being. Count on me to nurture you and your dreams. You are under my roof and under my protection. As long as I am able, I will not let anyone harm you. And I will never be a source of harm to you. With me, you are safe."

Wives, sons, and daughters around the world are hungry for this kind of active covering. Yet many men have walked off the job, either because they don't know how to provide covering, or because they selfishly refuse to give it. Imagine what would happen around the world if men embraced the call to active covering. Incest and rape statistics would fall immediately. Women would thrive in their unique gifts and callings. Insecure children would rise with confidence and no longer look to gangs and strangers for love. Teen drug use and teen sex, along with its related diseases and teen pregnancies, would decline to all-time lows. Men, we could start a revolution!

Passive covering is different, but perhaps as potent as active covering, especially given the numbers of women and children who have no male protection in a dangerous and predatory world. A man providing passive covering assumes a guardian role for any woman or child he encounters, anywhere, at any time. Passive covering calls on men to be consciously aware of the

I'm called as a husband and a father to assure my family, with pride, purpose, and action: "I will cover you, no matter what it takes. Count on me to provide for your needs. Count on me to look out for your physical, emotional, and spiritual well-being. Count on me to nurture you and your dreams."

signals we send. It calls on us to say, with our eyes, attitudes, words, and actions, "This is a safe place." It's about the aura we give off to women and children around us. Let's face it: Some men are creeps, because they're just plain creepy. Their lustful looks, crude words, inappropriate touches, and sexual aggression all contradict God's higher call for us to be protectors. Whether it's in the workplace, at the store, on an airplane, or in the church . . . creepy is creepy. And I've seen my share of creepy dudes who are anything but safe.

The man who is committed to passive covering chooses to walk in humble integrity. He strives to communicate to women and children, "You don't have to worry about me. My motives are pure. I don't want anything from you. Is there a way I can serve you?" And he means it!

Passive covering says to that single mom at church, "I respect your personal space and your emotional boundaries. You don't have to worry about me showing up at your home and encroaching on your 'safety zone' for some inappropriate reason. You don't have to worry if you come into my office alone; I'll leave, or leave the door open."

A man providing passive covering gives a warm hug, but a hug that doesn't linger and does not involve wandering hands. Passive covering is marked by eye contact, not by ogling breasts or anything else.

A man skilled in passive covering offers encouraging words to un-covered children--without making unnecessary and vain promises. Passive covering is all about posture, attitude, unselfishness, and a pure heart. Women and children are nurtured when they encounter the covering of a strong man with a pure and humble heart!

I serve as senior pastor at Messiah Community Church, and we regard our single women (many of whom are single mothers) as Crown Jewels. We are also grateful to have a congregation with a vibrant men's ministry. Our church is 43 percent men, and that percentage is growing. Our single women have come to deeply appreciate how Messiah's men provide a safe environment for them and their children. Our men keep a lookout for those church-hopping "vultures" who try to take advantage of single women. And we are very clear from the pulpit, "Do not come into our church and try to mess with our women and children. We will deal with you!"

Of course the single ladies would love to have more single men who are eligible for marriage, but they are grateful for a church full of men who refuse to leave them to the wolves. They are thriving because of the passive covering from Messiah's men.

Corrupted Covering

It's impossible to talk about covering without addressing the proverbial elephant in the room. With every "good and perfect gift coming down from the Father of the heavenly lights" (James 1:17) comes a sinister effort from the evil one. What God meant for good, the devil means for evil. As with every other beautiful and pleasing creation of God, Satan has sought to undermine the hospitable ways of God. Covering has come under fire in some painful and powerful ways, most notably through men adorned in the vestments of ministry, though not limited to them.

In recent years, the scandals of the Catholic Church and the cover-up at Penn State University (related to former assistant football coach Jerry Sandusky and university officials, including the legendary Joe Paterno) brought national attention to a horrible truth. Sometimes those who are responsible for nurturing and caring for the weakest among us abuse them instead. Men who were entrusted with the sacred authority of the priesthood and granted the trust of parents were consumed with their own lusts, using the cover of "helping vocation" to harm unsuspecting children and families. Both scandals are reminders that covering can be corrupted and that parents, especially fathers, must be vigilant and watchful, clarifying boundaries, and never giving an outsider an insider's seat in our children's lives.

A less obvious perversion of the good of covering is when a man assumes an *active covering* role in the lives of women and children who are not his own. At the very least, it's dysfunctional and confusing. Unmarried adults should avoid "playing house" with kids in their midst.

On another level it's unbiblical and suspicious. The apostle Paul sounded a warning about men who "worm their way into homes and gain control over gullible women, who are loaded down with sins and are swayed by all kinds of evil desires. . . ." (2 Timothy 3:6) A man attempting to be the *active covering* for a woman (and her children) should take the advice of Beyoncé. "Put a ring on it." To do otherwise is to send the wrong signals and to feed the insecurities and uncertainties of those who need the assurance of pure motives, unwavering commitment, and courageous male leadership. A woman and her kids do not need someone who comes and goes on a whim.

While writing this chapter, I received a call from a good friend who is an extraordinary NFL athlete. I've been coaching him and his fiancé as they move toward marriage. In recent conversations we've talked about the advantages and benefits of moving their wedding date back three months so they can work on some areas of their relationship. Both could see the benefits, but she would have to pick up her children and her life and move to another town. He's willing to cover her by letting her and the kids live in his home while they work toward the wedding date. He, in the meantime, would get an apartment. When they talked about all the things that would change as a result of their decision, including telling their guests and their wedding coordinator, things came to a head. The young woman became petrified at the thought of uprooting her life and all she's familiar with to re-locate where her husband-to-be lives and works.

She became hysterical, telling her fiancé, "Nothing I do seems to work! All my decisions seem to fall through. What if I get there and you decide you don't want me? I've given up my career for our relationship. I've changed my schooling in order to be home for my kids. What if you drop me after I leave everything I know?" (Her back-story is one of failed relationships with selfish and unfaithful men.)

As a teenager, she lived the "good life" with her mother and her boyfriend, whom she called "Dad." But that life was the life of a New York drug dealer. Eventually, "Dad," quit the drug game and went into music. That's when money got tight. The teen and her mom had to move to another town. From the age of 14 on, she had to work to help put food on the table. And "Dad," for whatever reason, never married her mother.

This girl's life changed dramatically when the romance ended. And she hasn't forgotten the sense of abandonment that came from corrupted covering.

Dangerous Covering

Finally, let me say a few words about *dangerous covering*. In the Old Testament, Abram made a major mistake when he took his wife Sarai's advice to sleep with her maidservant, Hagar. He opened a can of worms, which to this day is the source of much of the world's restlessness—specifically the lack of peace in the Middle East. When Sarai saw that her own maidservant looked at her with contempt after she'd given Abram the son he desperately wanted, someone had to go. Sarai refused to have anyone compete with her or her son for first place in Abram's life. So she "fixed" the problem by demanding that Abram send Hagar and her son, Ishmael, into the wilderness! It was hard to watch them leave, but Abram knew it was the only solution. No man can take care of two homes with two women! *Sister Wives* is a reality show, but it's anything but reality as it should be.

Men, it's dangerous (for many reasons) to try to cover any home other than your own. First of all, attempting to do so, even innocently, can stir the affections of a lonely woman and endanger your covenant commitment to your wife. Second, no woman in her right mind will share her husband with a single woman who "needs someone to fix her leaky faucet." Women know the pitfalls. Most men do too.

Let's take a closer look at the hypothetical situation in the preceding paragraph. Instead of heading over to the lonely woman's house, the man and his wife might decide to pay for a plumber's services. And the wife should make the arrangement with the sister in need. And don't forget about the church. It might have a ministry designed to meet needs like this one.

If neither solution is viable, men, stay home. Let God provide the plumber. Which reminds me: A man trying to actively cover a home other than his own is trying to play God in another woman's home. He's trying to be two places at the same time--emotionally, physically, and even spiritually. Any man who attempts to play God will find himself in *competition* with God. And we know how that always works out.

Covering is God's call for every man. But men are mandated by God to actively cover, protect, and provide for *only* our wives and children. Failure to do so makes us "worse than an infidel" (i.e., someone who rebels against God). (See 1 Timothy 5:8, KJV.)

So, men, let's provide a welcoming atmosphere of passive covering to every woman and child who graces us with her presence. But let's draw clear boundaries and avoid bringing pain or disappointment into vulnerable lives. Let's express godly, gracious, and pure intentions. Let's show people that God is near, even in a world that often feels unsafe.

Chapter 3 Instant Replay

1. Every man is called and created to provide covering.

2. There is appropriate covering, but there is also inappropriate covering, which is dangerous and sinful.

3. Any man who attempts to play God will find himself in *competition* with God. And we know how that always works out.

CHAPTER 4

Creating a Safe Place
(for Everyone)

4

The brutal 2012 gang-rape and murder of a 23-year-old Indian woman sparked a national and worldwide outcry. The case brought attention to an age-old problem in India. The culture has become a bastion of sexual harassment for men (like the seven rapists, whose number included the bus driver who was transporting the woman and her boyfriend.)

In a CNN interview, Indian-born model and TV personality Padma Lakshmi said of the tragedy, "It saddened me. It didn't surprise me, but it disgusted me."

Aggressive leering by men has become more than commonplace. It's the way things are, and it's downplayed as "Eve-teasing" or being playful. Padma experienced it first-hand during a recent trip to a New Delhi market with her cousin. She said, "We really felt intimidated. That happens every day. When I was growing up in India, I used to ride the bus to school, and I hated it. I *hated* it. I hated riding on a crowded bus. They [the men] would pinch you and grab you. You never feel safe."

The climate of misogyny and the denigration of women is not unique to India, of course. Protests against the sexual violence that took the Indian student's life spread to Nepal, Bangladesh, Pakistan, and Sri Lanka. Women stood up and proclaimed that they are tired of living in fear.

The message is spreading. Here in the United States, organizations like the International Justice Mission (IJM.org) have made it their mission to rescue young girls and women from sex trafficking and to help law enforcement agencies in Africa, Asia, and South America enforce local laws designed to protect women. According to The Rape Abuse & Incest National Network (RAINN.com), a national organization committed to fighting the abuse of women and children, a sexual assault happens every two minutes in America.

That's a shocking number, but keep in mind that an estimated 57 percent of rape and abuse cases go unreported. In the neighborhood where I grew up, women were beaten, badly and *routinely*. It was not routine, however, for someone to call the police. As a child, all the violence troubled me. However, it was normalized in our neighborhood. No one seemed especially alarmed—unless someone lost her life.

It makes me sad that I have to constantly remind my daughters that as beautiful, bright, and godly as they are, there are men--young and old--who have no regard for their bodies or their privacy. My two eldest daughters are students on the same college campus in Washington, D.C. (one is a senior, the other a sophomore). I remind them regularly, "Never walk alone on or around campus if it's dark, be aware of your surroundings, and keep your dorm doors locked when you're inside."

I don't let them drive the 55 miles from home to campus late at night. God forbid they have car trouble on the road!

Why the caution? During one two-week period at this college, two women were raped while studying in their dorms. The chief of the campus police explained (with grave disappointment) that the men who committed the sexual crimes were from the community around the campus. They targeted the dorms because of lax security.

Two young women have seen their lives forever changed. Not even a college campus in the nation's capitol is safe from men filled with sexual rage and selfish desires.

Two months after the rapes, I received a call from a member of my church. His friend was leaving a music lessons on another local college campus. It was routine; she'd being studying music there for years. But on this night, four males waited along the walkway as she made her way to her car. She said, "Good evening" and proceeded nervously. Two of them stepped in front of her and refused to move. They dragged her into a nearby alley. Three of them held her, while one at a time they raped her. By the grace of God, someone walked by the alley and these filthy and sad excuses for manhood ran off.

Today, this woman is devastated, confused, and afraid. Only by the grace of God will she ever recover her strength, dignity, and sanity.

These dangers are not new. Sexual aggression was as real in the ancient world of the Bible as it is today. The world has long been a dangerous place for women.

For example, Dinah, the only daughter of Jacob and Leah, was the victim of a man named Schechem's sexual aggression. Schechem, the son of the Hivite prince Hamor, just couldn't keep his hands to himself. Genesis 34:2 (KJV) tells us, "And when Shechem the son of Hamor the Hivite, the prince of the country, saw her [Dinah], he took her, and lay with her, and defiled her."

In 2 Samuel 13, Amnon, sick with urges to sleep with his own step-sister, Tamar, feigned sickness and then raped her. She was left shame-filled in her brother's house for the rest of her life. And her father, King David, did nothing to console her or to bring justice on her behalf.

Perhaps the most shocking narrative in the entire Bible is found in Judges 19. This passage tells of the heartless and violent rape of a young woman who was given over to her offenders by her father; her husband, who was a Levite (a minister); and an old man who had first offered her and her husband hospitality as they were traveling.

Note how the callousness in this story mirrors that of the men in India: "So the man took his concubine and sent her outside to them, and they raped her and abused her throughout the night, and at dawn they let her go. At daybreak the woman went back to the house where her master was staying, fell down at the door and lay there until daylight." (Judges 19:25-26)

There's more to this story, but I'll spare you the horrible details. You can read it in the Bible for yourself. The crux of the matter is this: Ever since sin entered the picture in Genesis 3, the world has been a dangerous place, period--especially for women and children.

The context of Judges 19 is that God's people had renounced His authority in their society and in their lives. Says the writer, "In those days Israel had no king. Everyone did as he saw fit." (Judges 21:25)

You see, it doesn't matter how great a nation is, economically or otherwise. When God's authority is spurned in that nation, state, city, neighborhood, or church, His covering is lifted.

Putting Locks on the Doors

Just because the world is a dangerous place for women doesn't mean that I have to be a dangerous "place" as a man. But many men are walking danger zones. They have no locks on the doors of their passions and desires. Nearly every woman whom many men see represents the potential for a fantasy-driven sexual encounter. For the past 14 years, I've worked with some NFL players who have honestly believed they are entitled to have anything or anyone they want. The concept of restraining their sexual passion is foreign to them.

> *A good man must learn to tell himself "no" when his urges scream "yes."*

But a good man must learn to tell himself "no" when his urges scream "yes." Otherwise, the destruction he will cause could last for generations.

When I tell men, "Put locks on your doors," I am challenging them (whether they are married or single) to become "safety zones" instead of "strike zones." I am calling them to be self-controlled and offer selfless protection to the women they encounter.

A man who is a "safety zone" makes a woman feel safe when she's around him. She doesn't have to worry about him looking at her sensually, touching her inappropriately, or speaking to her crudely. On the other hand, men who are "strike zones" give women that eerie, unsettled feeling. They have to watch themselves and stay on guard because, at any moment, a foul comment, ogling, or even an unwelcome grab is possible.

When the apostle Paul wrote to Titus about the young men under his pastoral care, he instructed, "Similarly, encourage the young men to be self-controlled." I think it's instructive what Paul did *not* tell Titus to teach: He didn't say, "Teach them to always dress to impress, to make sure their jeans look cool, to make sure they have a pocket full of money, to have the nicest car on the block, and to have swagger."

Paul spoke to the needs of young men with one word: self-control. Paul knew that if a guy learned self-control in his youth, he'd be set for life.

A man of self-control is sober-minded. He is diligent about the way he talks, behaves, advises others, and responds to life's circumstances. He has locks on his doors!

In contrast, a guy who lacks self-control is trouble waiting to happen. He is a pitfall to the unwary and unguarded. And, unless his mind is radically transformed by God's power, he will be self-centered, full of folly, indulgent, quick-tempered, and unteachable. He will be unable to cover a woman.

All of this is why self-control is the premier quality I look for in young men interested in dating my daughters. I'm watching to see how well a young man makes decisions. I notice how he maintains his car. Are the tires in good shape? How about the brakes? Do they squeak or grind when he drives up?

I also note how he manages his time, and whether his conversation is gracious and substantive. And, does he spend money wisely? Do his eyes roam whenever a good-looking woman walks by?

A man with locks on his doors is a safe bet and a safe place. I can trust him around my family. But one with no locks and no self-control will bring tears to a woman's eyes, heartache to a daughter's daddy, and even shame to a nation.

Re-Arranging Your Space

Dr. Samuel Chand is a dear friend and a gifted consultant to church and corporate leaders around the world. A few years ago, I invited him to speak at my church and to visit my office at the Baltimore Ravens training facility, where I was serving as team chaplain. He took one look at my office and said in his wonderful Georgian/East Indian accent, "Tell me what your job is as team chaplain."

I explained that my job was highly relational and that much of what I did was offer pastoral guidance and "soul care" to the players, coaches, staff, and their wives. I shared that much of my time was spent teaching and mentoring. Then he asked me a question I'll never forget: "Rod, if your job is to build relationships of trust and to offer counsel, why do you have your office arranged the way you do?"

He went on to note how my office was arranged to place me in a position of authority. It created a barrier between me and those who came in for counsel—or who were *thinking about* coming in. He wisely advised me that the players had enough authority figures to answer to. They had coaches, scouts, a general manager, a team owner, and so on.

Dr. Chand suggested that I rearrange the space by placing my desk against the wall and adding comfortable sectional seating so people could sit down and let down their guard as we talked.

Did I mention that Dr. Chand is brilliant? Oh, yes he is. I took his advice. At the next budget cycle, I added furniture to my ministry budget. The finance department thought I was crazy, but they approved it. I moved my desk to the corner, added three wide, cozy leather chairs, placed literature on a small round table. I replaced the harsh fluorescent lights with two lamps to create a warm glow. I can't begin to tell you how much traffic the renovation attracted to my office. Players, coaches, staff, and even visitors to the Ravens facility came in to sit with me, sometimes sharing their thoughts and needs for hours.

The new arrangement removed all kinds of barriers. It made people feel safe when they came in to talk with me.

I encourage men to incorporate Dr. Chand's advice to me in their own personal spaces—so that they can speak covering and safety to women. I tell them, "Re-arrange that space and how you function in it—especially when someone of the opposite sex is present."

When women encounter unfamiliar men in small spaces, like elevators or alone in an office or other building after work hours, they (rightly!) feel guarded.

By the way, "familiar" men should follow the same advice. We never know what hurtful experiences a woman brings with her when she is in our company. Changing a few things around can send a powerful message: "I'm safe. You don't have to worry when you're around me."

To begin, rather than greet a woman with a firm and close embrace, leave some space, some air, between the two of you. You might be the first guy with whom she's ever experienced such caution. I save the close hugs for the love of my life: my wife of 22 years. I've mastered the art of the one-arm hug and keeping the hand on the shoulder, never on the waist. Be careful not to allow a woman's breasts to touch you. (That's why that side-to-side hug is always safer.)

If you are in a room alone with a woman, always, always, always leave the doors open. I apply the Billy Graham Rule: Never counsel a woman alone. (Dr. Graham wouldn't even allow himself to be alone in a car with a woman who wasn't family.)

If I need to meet with a woman, I arrange to have someone else in the building with me, and I leave the door open. If your work requires meeting colleagues who are women, meet them in public spaces, like a coffee shop or the company dining area. Putting a table between the two of you establishes safe space. And let your wife know the meeting is on your calendar.

If in an elevator, I say hello with a smile and politely look forward, not at a woman's cleavage or legs. It's not a bad idea to take a slight step away from her. One slight step toward a woman in that situation can make her nervous.

I know all of this sounds like over-kill. It might be. But *intentionality* is the name of the game here. We're talking about creating covering, an environment of safety for the women who share our space. I've shared some suggestions, but the key is to do *whatever* it takes. And if you've read this far, it's probably safe to assume that your heart is to be "that kind of guy." So go overboard. Re-arrange the space. Make it feel safe.

Chapter 4 Instant Replay

1. The world can be a dangerous place for women and children--physically, emotionally, and psychologically.

2. Many women suffer harm from the men they trust to protect them—husbands, fathers, brothers, co-workers, and the like.

3. Men should go overboard to make all the women in their lives feel safe and secure.

CHAPTER 5
You're the Man for the Job!

5

To say that covering and protecting are part of God's natural design for men can seem like an affront to a culture of gender equality. In a culture where many women are the bread-winners, whether they are married or single, it can sound foolish to say they need a man to cover them. Many women in our society, including my amazing mom, have been required to hold down a job, raise kids, and keep the home running smoothly without the help and support of a man. There are women who serve in the military, lead companies of all sizes, and who can protect themselves from just about anyone. They are anything but weak. They don't need a condescending man to "fix things" for them.

However, a man who dignifies and esteems a woman, values her strengths, and compliments her natural gifts (with pure motives) understands what covering is all about. When God delivered Eve to Adam, his first words oozed awe, respect, and amazement:

"This is now bone of my bones

And flesh of my flesh;

She shall be called Woman,

Because she was taken out of Man."

(Genesis 2:23 NKJV)

Adam was wonder-struck at God's creative power and artistic skill. Eve, too, was made in God's image, and Adam quickly recognized her to be his equal—a feminine version of himself. She was indeed the partner he could not find among any of the creatures God had provided. Sure, Eve was his wife, but the principle of covering is found in his attitude and approach to her. He dignified her and accepted her without hesitation. It was his natural response, because God had built Adam to cover.

Before Adam and Eve sinned, male dominance, neglect, abuse, and abandonment were nowhere to be found. They were not even whispered about or imagined. It wasn't until sin entered the picture that covering protection was subtracted from the equation of male-female relationships. The trouble started when Adam neglected his responsibility to guard the Garden of Eden from the serpent who enticed Eve. As soon as Eve ate the forbidden fruit, animosity and competition began to pollute their relationship. Adam and Eve started playing The Blame Game. Ever since, misunderstanding, tension, mistrust, and fear have become sad realities of male-female relationships.

The Bible is full of examples: Abram blew it with Sarai out of fear for his own well-being. Rahab had to find a way to fend for herself and her family when the spies came to Jericho. (Where were the men in her life?) Abigail had to cover her husband, Nabal, whose foolishness almost got everyone around him killed. The prophet

Malachi wrote of men who discarded their faithful wives for younger, pagan wives who piqued their male curiosity.

Indeed, a male-female relationship does not come pre-loaded with peace, protection, respect, and honor. We have to work to build these qualities. And only through the power of Christ at work in both sexes can such life-giving relationship dynamics be developed.

> *A male-female relationship does not come pre-loaded with peace, protection, respect, and honor. We have to work to build these qualities.*

In the beginning, as I've noted, things were different. Adam covered Eve. It was innate to his make-up, and it flowed flawlessly in their relationship as man and woman. She received his covering. It was a natural expression of his being made in God's image. Adam was simply being the man God created him to be. He provided covering to Eve by honoring her, esteeming her, accepting her, and giving her dignity. He had a clear sense of Eve's worth. Simply put, she was made in the image of God. Her worth was not in question or up for debate. Until sin ruined things, Adam was on the job. His God-given job.

And just as Adam was the man for the job, so are we—today's men. It's time to rediscover the truth that we have what it takes. We will have to work hard, but we can bring male/female relationships back into harmony. Something in society will be set aright when men around the world begin to celebrate women for the glory of God in them. Single women will feel less vulnerable and more valuable. Wives will flourish emotionally. Daughters will feel confident and beautiful. Co-workers will be treated fairly and find the hope of opportunity rather than glass ceilings above them. And mothers will feel encouraged to pour their lives into their children, their homes, and their husbands. All because of the renewed outlook and disposition of men who are intentional about covering.

The Keys to Covering

It's time to get practical. What does covering look like? I've found five things that the women in my life need from me and the other men in their lives. Whether it's my wife, my daughters, my mother, my staff, or my friends, five things seem to resonate with them. Obviously, not all five apply to every male-female relationship. But there is an expectation that a brother, husband, father, or college classmate will be able to offer at least one of these, in the appropriate circumstances:

- Physical Protection

- Financial Provision

- Emotional Support

- Spiritual Leadership

- Relational Fidelity

I will go into each one of these in further detail later in the book, but for now, let's deal with them briefly.

Physical Protection

Growing up without the presence of my dad in the home was tough for me. As I've said, my mom was capable as the provider.

By the grace of God, she kept food on the table and clothes on the backs of three growing boys. But the night someone broke into our apartment and took her nice jewelry and the color TV, we all felt vulnerable. Though we were not home when the burglary took place, we felt violated. I was only nine years old, but I knew the sight of fear when I saw it. My five-foot-two-inch mom was shaken, angry, and uncertain--all at the same time. Her home had been unlawfully entered, and there was no man there to speak calm into the situation or to assure us that he would handle any future intruders.

After the incident, I made a club by wrapping black electrical tape around an 18-inch metal bar. I put a small piece of rope on the end, mimicking a policeman's billy club. I told my mom, "If anybody comes into the house while I'm gone, you take this club and knock 'em out! Then call the police."

Mom didn't laugh at me. She hugged me and thanked me for being willing to do whatever I could to protect her. She knew I couldn't really protect her, physically. But she honored the "man" that was rising up in her baby boy. He longed to protect her from intruders, thieves, and violators of any kind. She welcomed the protector in me. After all, what woman desires and celebrates a man who has no courage to stand in the gap physically, when necessary?

Financial Provision

Let's restate the obvious: Women are fully capable of earning healthy incomes to sustain their families and maintain their homes. Thank God for a nation where women are increasingly being granted their rights to fair and equal wages! I know many women who earn a great living. Lots of them make more money than their husbands.

They do not depend on a man for their financial well-being, and I wouldn't suggest otherwise.

What I do suggest, however, is that a man *should* be capable of and willing to provide for his household. A wife shouldn't have to wonder whether her husband is ever going to get himself "together enough" to take care of the household's financial needs. She shouldn't have to give him monthly pep talks, telling him he's capable of making more money or begging him to respond to the Craigslist ad she found.

A daughter shouldn't have to feel like she is a burden to her father when she needs twenty bucks to buy a uniform for the school concert. A cashier at our local Ross store took note when my daughters thanked me for taking them shopping for school clothes. "You're lucky," she told them. "My father complains if I ask him for ten dollars."

I've met too many women whose husbands or fathers were financially capable to provide for various needs--but they were too selfish to do so.

A woman who must always bear the burdens of family financial responsibility cannot truly respect a man who could and should be shouldering his share of the load. And no daughter brags about a dad who groans every time she asks him to meet her financial needs.

Emotional Support

Another key to covering a woman involves giving emotional support. That's tough for most men. Most of us aren't wired that way. We can give advice. We can give money. We can even tell you our opinion--assuming our favorite team is not playing on television at the moment. But walking with a woman emotionally requires that men access a reservoir that most of us have yet to tap. I ran into a colleague in Starbucks the other day. He's a well-known sports reporter who has excelled at his craft. But he confirmed my theory. As we were discussing the busy-ness of life, with work and teenage kids, he lamented, "Girls are so much more difficult to raise when they hit puberty. I don't know what to do. I can't make sense of all the emotions and how to deal with them."

I told my colleague that the first step is simply asking. My wife tells me that she feels emotionally supported when she has my undivided attention (i.e., no computers, no books, and no television) and I am listening to what she's sharing with me. My girls say they feel emotionally supported when I show up at their dance recitals and other school events. And they love getting a text from Daddy or even a hug when they feel that life is falling to pieces in their world!

Sometimes, emotional support simply means letting a woman or a teenage daughter feel what she's feeling--without making cynical remarks when we don't understand.

Emotional support can mean so many things, but ultimately it means appreciating and respecting a woman's emotional make-up, even though it's worlds apart from a man's ultra-rational tendencies. A woman who feels free to be herself and free to express her emotions will have confidence to face any challenge in her path.

Spiritual Leadership

If a man's going to cover a woman, he had better get on his game spiritually! But that goal is not as complicated as most men make it. Simply put, a man must be unafraid to connect with God in a meaningful way, even if this is new to him. A woman loves to see a man rally himself and the family to church on Sunday mornings. He doesn't have to know all the church lingo, be able to quote chapters of Scripture, or pray using five-syllable words. For starters, he just needs to do something more spiritually vital than sit and read the Sunday morning paper. Most of the women I know will applaud a man who makes worship a priority. They find spiritual leadership attractive.

When trouble hits (and it will hit at some point), a man who is willing to bow his knees in prayer, read the Scriptures, and remind his woman that God is going to see them through is offering spiritual cover. Those prayers don't have to be long and complicated, either. Just talking to God about the situation brings comfort and calm to a woman. I believe it alerts dark spiritual forces that someone is standing in the gap on her behalf, making it difficult for them to attack her successfully.

I encourage men to start small. Rome was not built in a day, but somebody had to get the work started. As a pastor, it's been amazing to watch families turn from the brink of divorce and disaster. Men who used to watch every Sunday morning pre-game program, and then a bunch of games, decided to bring their families to church. And now their relationships with the wives and children have taken a significant turn for the better--all because of one simple act of spiritual leadership.

Wide receiver Anquan Boldin was a key player on the 2013 Ravens Super Bowl team. He is married to Dionne, his high school sweetheart. Discussing his marriage he says, "Dionne, and

I pray together, and that is a key for us as a couple. It's part of our communication with each other, and it helps ensure that we are on the same page."

Relationship Fidelity

During our 2013 march to the Super Bowl, one of the Ravens players became embroiled in very public battle with the mother of his children. The couple wasn't married at the time, but they were raising children together (not an arrangement I recommend). I got a phone call from this mom. She was "through with the relationship," she told me. She was leaving and never returning. She'd had enough of seeing marriage dangled in front of her like a carrot, while "he does his thing."

She left the household, hired a lawyer, and began the proceedings for child support and custody. Oh, it was ugly.

Meanwhile, this player was a mess at work. He wasn't defensive; he admitted his wrong behavior. But the thought of losing his children and the woman he deeply loved and needed was destroying him inside. He didn't know if she would come back to him, so he began to pray about the situation.

Meanwhile, I counseled him, "Stop playing around with God, and stop playing around with her. She's sick and tired of being your 'baby mama' and convenient live-in lover. She wants to be your wife."

No one following this couple's story gave them a chance of salvaging the relationship. They'd been down this same road, publicly, before. Only this time was worse.

He said to me, "Rev, if she comes back to me, I'm going to marry her."

I replied, "If she comes back to you, it'll be a miracle from God!"

And what do you know? She came back. He married her, abandoned his wild living, followed through on his commitments to grow in Christ, and made her the priority she deserved to be.

I've never seen that young woman happier, calmer, and more excited about her life. All she wanted was to be the only one. She wanted the covering of relational fidelity!

What Difference Does Covering Make?

God doesn't give us haphazard assignments. He never calls a man to do anything that doesn't have meaning and the potential for significant, positive impact. Just as God brought order to the chaos-filled sphere we call earth by delineating day from night and separating water into sky and sea, He called Adam to keep order in the Garden. Through God-honoring relationship, creativity, and work, Adam would keep things as God intended them. Adam's role was to keep Eden the sanctuary God had created it to be. When a man fulfills his call to cover, he makes home, work, church, and even the "playground" feel like sanctuaries of God's presence. In these sanctuaries, people flourish and find the opportunity to be all God intends them to be.

Our duty to cover is a significant assignment with extraordinary implications. Men have been given the keys to covering, just as Jesus gave Peter the keys to the church kingdom. We can unlock amazing potential in people's lives. We can help bring out the best in our daughters, our sisters, our friends, our wives, and even our co-workers. But if we misuse the keys or fail to use them at all, we can make a mess of the lives God desires to bless. When we deviate from our masculine duties, the consequences can be devastating.

Men, God has given us extraordinary influence on girls and women in all walks of life. We can't afford to abdicate or disregard our unique calling and responsibility any longer. There's too much at stake. Committed men who take the call to cover seriously make a huge difference in lives.

According to Dr. Tim Clinton, a respected Christian psychologist and author, seven out of 10 teenage girls believe they're not "good enough." They don't feel they measure up to the standard of who they should be. Sixty-two percent say they're insecure and unsure of themselves. Fifty-seven percent of teen girls have a mother who criticizes her appearance. Seventy-one percent of them believe that their appearance doesn't measure up, in terms of physical beauty or style trends.

Girl-on-girl bullying is growing at an alarming rate. All of these facts are symptoms of much deeper social, relational, and emotional issues. I'm not saying men are at the root of these problems, but I do maintain that men who are willing to offer covering to their daughters, nieces, and neighbors can reverse the negative trends. A man who is pure in heart can be a voice of unconditional affirmation. He can ignite a spark of confidence in a girl's soul.

The tragedy of poor self-esteem and shrinking confidence takes its toll on ladies of all ages. Many of them are simply looking for love and approval, but they aren't sure what these qualities truly look like. And they don't know where to find them. And if a woman cannot find approval in a good-hearted person, she follows a familiar path. She finds something else to ease the pain and fill the void. Often, that "something" is drugs. Or it might be self-harm, alcohol, or an abusive relationship.

As chaplain of the Ravens and through my experiences with other NFL teams, I've watched teenage girls and mothers cry out emotionally for their fathers and husbands. It's not necessarily a vocal cry, but it sure is loud. One teen I know simply couldn't figure out where she was headed in life. I'd watched her change from a vibrant little girl of 10 into a high school junior who was awkward in her appearance and uncertain where she fit in. I suggested to her dad, a member of the coaching staff, that he spend more time with her. I told him, "She's crying out for your attention."

This coach resented what he called my "unprofessional counsel," and he stopped coming to team chapel services and Bible studies.

Later, he divorced his wife and left a college-bound son and two daughters drifting in a sea of confusion, anger and resentment.

His wife later told me, "Rod, you were right. All that these kids and I wanted was him. But he was busy making money, a career, and a name for himself."

What a difference that husband and dad would have made had he taken his assignment to cover seriously!

This brings to mind another coach I got to know. His wife and daughters lived in one place, while he traveled from one team to another, living apart from his family so that he could coach big-time pro athletes.

One morning, I bumped into him at a Starbucks. He was having coffee with a beautiful, buff woman who was not his wife. Obviously surprised to see me, he introduced her as his housekeeper. (He changed "housekeepers" a few times during his years in Baltimore.)

Later, he told me that he was having trouble with his 15-year-old daughter. She was rebelling--using drugs, seeing older guys, and struggling in school.

Soon after, I met this man's wife. She began to call me occasionally, expressing her concern that her husband was having affairs. As I got to know this couple better, I offered them counsel.

"Your daughter is acting out," I told each of them. "She wants her daddy, and life won't be right in her world until she has consistent time with him."

Not surprisingly, every time this teen visited her father in Baltimore--or he left the job to spend time at home--the family situation improved.

Unfortunately, this dad was a serial adulterer. Eventually, he took a coaching job in another city. He made even more money, but his family endured more suffering. The teen daughter took a baby-sitting job for a former NFL player, who was twice her age. He sexually abused her. He went to prison, where he is serving hard time (up to 20 years), but the damage has been done. Who knows what kind of internal trauma that girl has suffered?

The bigger question is, "How different would the story have been if this teen had been covered appropriately, both by her dad and her employer?"

A few nights ago, I attended my youngest daughter's high school dance recital. I took note of three pairs of young girls. Each pair was holding hands, hugging, and generally acting like silly "bubble gum" lovers. One member of each couple seemed "damaged" and suffering from low self-esteem. The other girl projected a more masculine aura. But beneath the projected confidence, I could see awkwardness. In each face, I could see pain caused by a man. The look on their beautiful faces said, "I'll never let another man hurt me again—even if I have to act like a man myself."

I know that what I have just written will be unpopular with some readers. But please don't misunderstand me. I am not attacking any group of people. I am simply maintaining that when men cover the young women in their lives and set healthy boundaries, they protect self-esteem and self-confidence. And they help young girls avoid casual sexual experimentation—as well as experimentation with drugs, alcohol, self-harm, and so on.

The disconnection of many fathers from their sons and daughters is pandemic, and we are reaping worldwide consequences. As former All-Pro lineman Matt Birk puts it, "Our current culture is 100-percent at odds with our faith in God."

God's concern for this problem is poignantly expressed through the prophet Malachi: "See, I will send you the prophet Elijah before that great and dreadful day of the Lord comes. He will turn the hearts of the fathers to their children, and the hearts of the children to their fathers; or else I will come and strike the land with a curse." (Malachi 4:5-6)

In other words, if fathers and father figures don't reconnect with their children, guide them, and cover them, there will be social, relational, and emotional upheaval everywhere. Don't believe me? Just pick up a newspaper or click on one of the news channels.

Discerning women know that I am not exaggerating. Many of them know firsthand the impact of being around men--fathers, husbands, brothers, co-workers, employers, uncles, and others-- who are clueless about covering.

Others know the other side of the proverbial coin--the positives of being covered by caring men of integrity. These women are confident. Life is less stressful for them. They are not desperate for love. They feel like someone has their back in what can be a vicious world. They don't feel compelled to accept offers from the first "low bidder" who comes to consume rather than invest in a relationship. They respect themselves, and they have a healthy regard for men.

They don't regard men as oppressors or as unnecessary baggage on life's journey. They know that both genders have something vital to bring to life.

Chapter 5 Instant Replay

1. Covering is a biblical calling of manhood.

2. Women who are covered—at home, at work, and in the church—thrive as they seek to fulfill their God-given purpose.

3. Women who are covered respect themselves, and they have a healthy attitude toward men.

CHAPTER 6

Understanding Women

6

Let's face it: Most men do not understand women. We love them, we need them, and we want them. Understanding them is another matter. We find their beauty, their charm, and even their bodies mystifying. Many men wander through life baffled. They shake their heads as if to say, "Oh my goodness! I'll never figure women out!"

Dr. A.R. Bernard, the great pastor and community leader of Christian Cultural Center in Brooklyn, New York, says he's found the secret to women. "They don't know what they want," he says, "but they do know what they *don't* want."

Seriously, though, there's a serious message embedded in Dr. Bernard's quip: Unless a man understands how a woman is made and how she thinks, it will be difficult for him to embrace his call to cover her. And understanding involves knowing a woman's fears as well as her hopes, her dislikes as well as her likes.

When God crafted Eve out of Adam's rib, He did not consult with him. God didn't ask Adam, "What do you think she should look like, sound like, and be like?" He didn't ask Adam to submit a blueprint.

Adam had no idea what was coming. God put him to sleep, and then God went to work! (Genesis 2:21) The Lord crafted, with artistic excellence, a whole new being who was like the man—yet quite different in many ways. How long did Adam have to search for the words he used to describe Eve: "This is now bone of my bones. . . ."

One gets the sense that Adam was blown away, in the best possible sense. Here was a mysterious being unlike anything he'd ever seen, yet she perfectly complemented his own nature.

One reason that life in the Garden was so beautiful is that Adam didn't fully understand Eve, but he didn't reject or resist her. He didn't expect her to be an exact replica of himself. She didn't have to think like he did, talk like he did, or act like he did. After all, what would be the point of *that*?

I know what some of you are thinking: Things have changed since the Fall. That is true, but we should never forget the way things were supposed to be. We shouldn't lose sight of God's ideal.

Men, we might not fully grasp the mind and heart of women, but we should still accept them fully. Women were made in God's awesome image, just as we were. What we cannot understand, we can still respect. We don't have to understand the shifts in her emotions, but we can still love and respect her. We don't have to understand why she wants one more pair of shoes, but we can accept that she likes shoes. We don't have to understand why she wants a heart-to-heart conversation at the same moment we just want to chill and watch some TV. But we can honor her preference as legitimate, not as a nuisance.

Remember, Adam received Eve and embraced her fully as a gift from God. If women need nothing else from men, they need to feel accepted, appreciated, and applauded for who God has made them to be.

So, one more time: Men, let's respect, even when we do not agree. Let's embrace and enjoy the fascinating mystery of the female gender.

The Power of a Woman

In the Garden, Adam knew God's voice. It was familiar to him, and it resonated with him. Likewise, the animals knew Adam's voice. They came and went at his command.

> *If women need nothing else from men, they need to feel accepted, appreciated, and applauded for who God has made them to be.*

But Eve brought a new voice to the world. Before he met his soul-mate, Adam had heard only two voices—God's and his own. When Eve first spoke, I believe Adam quaked. I imagine that he felt chills down his spine when he heard the first melodic tones from Eve. I bet he got goose bumps.

If you've ever been in love, you know the power of a woman's voice. And if you're a dad, you know there's nothing like hearing your daughter call you "Daddy."

That one word can melt a heart as hard as stone. It can even get a dad to pry a few bills out of his wallet at the mall!

Of course, there's a dark side to this power. Every year men spend millions of dollars on phone sex. Faceless strangers with fake names have men all over the world addicted to their voices.

Some people argue that a woman's power over a man rests in her body, her physical sensuality. To a degree, that is true. But I argue that a woman's body and sensuality are extensions of her voice.

It's intriguing that the Bible says nothing about the physical appearance of Delilah, the woman who brought down the powerful Samson. It was her words that did the deed. I've seen powerful men wreck their marriages, families, and careers for women who were not drop-dead gorgeous.

Gary Kubiak, head coach of the Houston Texans, warns his players about "Delilah women." "They are undefeated," he says. "They have brought down kings. They have brought down great men."

And it's not mere physical beauty that does the trick. It's not only the words she says. It's *how* she says them that affects men so dramatically.

If she says something the right way, a woman can get a man to do just about anything--good or bad.

I have to wonder, "What exactly did Monica Lewinsky say to President Bill Clinton that made him willing to risk an entire presidency and the security of a nation?"

Conversely, Rahab (whom we met earlier) saved her entire family because she knew how to talk to people in power—to the king of Jericho and to the spies Joshua sent to investigate the city. She used the power of her voice to redirect the destructive efforts of a king and to strike a deal with the spies. (See Joshua 1:1-21.) It's no wonder she's in the lineage of Jesus.

Here's another example from later in the Old Testament: Abigail couldn't control her husband Nabal's loose tongue, but she used her own voice to convince the powerful David to control his temper and to spare Nabal's life. Samuel records these words from her encounter with David, the angry king-to-be: She fell at his feet and said: "Pardon your servant, my lord, and let me speak to you; hear what your servant has to say." (1 Samuel 25:24)

Yes, Abigail also brought some gifts for David, but her *words* persuaded him to re-think his deadly intentions.

David was so captivated by her wisdom and the gentleness of her voice. It was only after Abigail spoke that David accepted her gifts. Then he told her, "Go up in peace to your house. See, I have heeded your voice and respected your person." (1 Samuel 25:35 NKJV)

Esther, too, maximized the moment when she was invited into the presence of King Artaxerxes. She measured her words. (See Esther 5:7-8.) Yes, her good looks got her in the door, but it was her voice in the king's ear that God used to save her people. Never underestimate the power of a woman's voice!

This brings us back to Eve. Eve wielded unusual power in the Garden. She was the only other being created in God's image. She'd been placed alongside Adam to be his helper. Her suggestions for operating the Garden effectively were vital to its flourishing. Adam was wise to listen to his wife. Her God-given gifts helped Adam be at his best.

But the influence that made Eve an asset also made her a liability. Her voice brought Adam's downfall—and the ruination of all they had enjoyed together.

When she offered him the forbidden fruit, he listened to her voice. God later rebuked Adam because he "listened to your wife and ate fruit from the tree about which I commanded you, 'You must not eat from it,' "Cursed is the ground because of you; through painful toil you will eat food from it all the days of your life." (Genesis 3:17)

It's important to understand Adam's mistake. He listened to the voice of God's gift to him when that voice contradicted the voice of God, the gift-giver Himself.

The power of a woman's voice works for good when she harnesses her words for good, under God's authority. That's why the devil does all he can to rob women of their voices--through rape, incest, abuse, neglect, abandonment, and so on. He knows where her strength lies.

If you're going to be a man of covering, encourage the ladies you know to submit their voices to God and to use them for His glory and the good of others. Remind them that they can save nations and change destinies. Invite their views and perspectives, and appreciate that a woman's voice is different from a man's. She has something to say--something the world needs to hear.

When a woman's words align with God's Word, everybody who hears her voice will be richly blessed.

The Making of a Woman

When God made woman, He knew exactly what He was doing. Adam needed a mate--someone suitable to help him and to be a companion to him. If a man doesn't know the ABCs of a woman's design, covering will never make sense to him. God made Eve in response to Adam's need and as a complement to his lonely life.

Remember, Eve was not created from dirt, as Adam was. She was crafted from Adam's removed rib. And God gave her things He didn't give Adam. She had the ability to bear children. He made her body differently, with great care and purpose. God did not make her haphazardly.

Here is a truth vital to understanding women. Eve was made in response to Adam's need. That means that we men *need* women. It's not just a matter of desire. God surveyed all of creation and pronounced everything "good." With one exception: When He saw Adam without a mate, He said, "It is not good."

A man who thinks he doesn't need a woman is kidding himself-- even if that woman is a sister who gives him a different perspective or a mother who cooks his favorite meal occasionally and shares her life wisdom with him. No man was made to be alone, not even the most devout and pious servant of God. Admitting our need for women corrects a twisted sense of superiority and calls us to regard women, humbly, as vital to our survival. A wise man knows he's only as good as the woman by his side.

Because Eve was made in response to Adam's need, she was the answer to his question, the missing link in his chain, and the final piece to his puzzle. A woman's personality and her purpose are responsive in nature. Women respond deeply to a man's suggestions, affirmations, and criticisms. Sometimes, they respond to their own detriment.

For example, many women trapped in the prison of prostitution have revealed that their fathers' words and actions are responsible. I've heard lots of comments like the following:

"He told me I was fat and that I'd never amount to anything."

"He began molesting me when I was young, so I decided I was not worth loving."

"He left when I was six, and I assumed it was my fault."

Conversely, when a woman is fed positive words, she responds quite differently. A father should tell his girls they're beautiful every day. He'll see beauty burst forth from their souls. A husband should tell his wife how much better his life is with her than without—then watch her response. The meals will get better, the house will be cleaner, and the sex just might become more frequent! Women are made to respond. And they will . . . for better or worse.

Of all the parts God could have used to build Eve, He chose the rib of Adam. I've been around NFL football players who've suffered bruised and broken ribs. It's a game changer--one of the most excruciating and painful injuries a person can suffer. You can't breathe deeply. You can't sleep comfortably. And heaven forbid you laugh or cough!

Until a rib heals, it's tender to the slightest touch.

Men, we should let the story of Eve's creation remind us that if we want a good woman by our sides, we must be willing to pay a painful price and lose a part of our selves. If we're going to encourage our girls to become wonderful women, we sometimes have to "take one for the team." Eve was presented to Adam to help him—but not to make life perpetually convenient and pain-free.

Some men want the woman to make all the sacrifices. But covering requires us to be willing to sacrifice: our time, our agendas, our resources, and our egos. Covering requires that we give up a part of ourselves, and that we be willing to experience a bit of discomfort from time to time.

What a Woman Needs

All this brings us to a woman's needs. Contrary to what most men think, women don't need as much as we think they do. As a sports chaplain and as a pastor, I've ministered to families all over the country. I've talked with girlfriends, daughters, and wives representing a wide variety of professions, ethnicities, personalities, income levels, and more. But they all say the same things. They have a core need to be valued and to feel secure. Yes, they want to feel beautiful and special. They want to be loved. And all of this, and more, comes to a woman who is valued and made to feel secure.

When a woman is treasured as precious in the sight of a man (her daddy, her husband, or her boyfriend), a glowing fire of confidence burns inside her. Expensive engagement rings are popular for good reason. They make women feel valued. Now, I'm all for a man sacrificing to buy his bride-to-be that five-carat engagement ring. But, frankly, it can be a false statement of value. There are men who can afford to spend the money on a big rock, but they won't spend time out of their busy schedules to take a walk or have a meaningful conversation over a cup of coffee.

A few years ago, the wife of an NFL coach told me, "I threw the thirty-thousand-dollar ring at him and left our marriage, because I got tired of being alone!"

This woman didn't want the big ring. She wanted *him*. She wanted to feel truly valued. She wanted the marriage to be more important than the job.

This couple divorced, but they have learned from their mistakes and are building a great friendship. They are talking about remarriage. His current coaching job is not as demanding as the previous one. They spend time together, talking on the phone and going on dates when they can. She's a new woman now.

This brings us to a woman's need to feel secure. Guys, that lady in your life needs to know that no one else holds the spot in your life that she does. Your wife wants that special place. So does your daughter. My three daughters all need to know there is a spot in my heart that is uniquely theirs. Each of our relationships is special.

As for my wife and me, what we share together, no one else in the universe shares.

Each of the Hairston women gets regular dates alone with me. It's her special time with me and mine with her.

My wife and daughters eat this up. They feel rejuvenated when we've gone to a movie, or to a concert, or enjoyed a cup of coffee together. I've been doing it for years. Now they won't let me *not* do it!

That's why women who value themselves never settle for being with a man who cannot be faithful to one woman. Infidelity on any level strikes a chord of *dis-ease* in a woman. It can rob her of confidence and peace of mind. A woman whose sense of security has been violated is not her best self.

I've seen women lose too much weight, gain too much weight, and worry too much. I've seen the light go out of their eyes. They no longer thrive; they merely survive. Some women tolerate cheating for years, but after a while a switch shuts off in them and they detach emotionally from the relationship, even if they stay physically. Cheating turns a woman's world upside down--until she re-discovers her worth, walks away, and determines never to settle for less.

If a man is the covering kind, he'll do all he can to make a woman feel valued and secure. A little time and commitment can go a long way, impacting generations of women-in-the-making. Imagine what could happen in a family, in a community, in a church, in a city, even in a nation where men really endeavor to understand women and seek to honor their essential needs for value and security. We'd start a covering revolution and turn the world around!

Chapter 6 Instant Replay

1. Most men are baffled by women; they don't know what makes them tick.

2. Guys, that lady in your life needs to know that no one else holds the spot in your life that she does!

3. If a man is the covering kind, he will do all he can to make a woman feel valued and secure.

4. A wise man knows he's only as good as the woman by his side.

When A Woman Needs You Physically (Physical Covering)

7

In my 22 years of collegiate and NFL chaplaincy, I discovered a powerful principle that made my ministry to world-class athletes and coaches effective. It's what I call "strategic presence." Strategic presence is placing yourself in the right place at the right time in order to care for people effectively. No one can be everywhere at all times, except the omnipresent God of the universe. So, to encourage athletes and gain the privilege of influencing their lives, I would show up, physically, at strategic times.

In Baltimore, for example, I'd visit one or two practices a week. I'd provide a chapel service the night before the game or on game-day morning, to bring calm before the storm of competition. I'd pray with Coach John Harbaugh in his office, just after team warm-ups. Then, the players and I would gather in the center of the locker room for pre-game prayer, just minutes before their on-field introductions.

If a player was injured on the field, I'd hop on the Gator Cart and ride to the x-ray room with him. If a player had to be transported to a hospital, I'd be in the ambulance with him. For me, strategic presence meant being there physically, even if I didn't say much.

The players welcomed it and depended on it. I couldn't be at every practice, or every birthday party, or every community event, but I tried to be physically present when I could. As a dad or a husband, you can do the same thing.

In every lady's life there are key times when she needs to know her man will be there. Not in spirit, in word, or by Skype. In *person*.

I understand that we are sometimes required to be on the road. And sometimes we have to work long days and long nights. But sometimes we must make hard decisions so that we can be physically present to provide strategic covering to someone we love.

Let's look at a few examples:

When the Bills Are Due

A man's physical presence is vital is when the bills are due. Water bills, the rent, the mortgage, tuition, grocery bills, and the like come due regularly, cyclically. There's no getting around them. Jesus said, "In this life you will have trouble." He could have easily added, "And bills." Bills represent the physical needs of a family. And if a man wants to give his girls a clear sense that they are covered, he'd better step up and make sure the bills get paid. No woman wants to hear a man say, "I'm so in love with you and so committed to you" when he doesn't take care of the bills. Those words mean nothing when the house has gone into foreclosure!

> *In every lady's life there are key times when she needs to know her man will be there. Not in spirit, in word, or by Skype. In person.*

I understand that the man isn't always the one who writes the checks or makes the electronic-funds transfers in his home, but he should have a system and the financial resources in place to ensure that basic household expenses are being covered.

It's not pretty when a man neglects his physical covering duties. I once watched a player turn away, physically, from his new (and newly pregnant) wife. It was painful to watch this young man, who professed faith in Christ, fail to cover the wife he had begged God for. They met online, dated for a year, and decided to get married. This woman was not a "gold-digger." She'd been saving herself for the man of her dreams. At age 26, she thought she'd found him. She moved to Baltimore after the wedding, and into the home he'd purchased for them. She did everything she could to be an asset to her new husband in his demanding football career. She cooked, took care of home, and took care of *him*.

Unfortunately, this player's caring for his new household upset his mother. She expected him to keep paying her bills as well. She was jealous, and the picture that developed wasn't pretty. Eventually, this man caved to his mother's pressure. For nearly a month, he abandoned his new wife—left her alone in an unfamiliar neighborhood in a new city. He told her he wouldn't return until she was gone. Meanwhile, she learned she was pregnant.

It's important to note that this newlywed had left behind a well-paying job, her family, and a happy life back in Florida—all to be with her new husband and support his career. Now she was totally un-covered, except for the roof over her head and the members of my church who walked alongside her.

Things got worse before they got better. The player, his mother, and his stepfather all decided the young wife needed to pack her bags and disappear. They devised a plan to pressure her to exit the property. One unpaid bill at a time, they sabotaged her.

First, the player stopped paying the cable TV bill, so the service was cut off. Next, he blocked her access to the bank accounts. As a result, this young pregnant woman struggled to buy food.

Then, the stepfather crept into the home late one night, went into the basement, and shut off the water. Eventually, the electricity bills went unpaid, and that service was cut off as well.

I realize that some readers might think I'm making up this story, or at least exaggerating. You might find it hard to imagine such cowardice and cruelty. Sadly, this story is completely true. I've actually omitted some horrific details.

Eventually, this young woman's grandmother traveled from Florida to Baltimore to help her granddaughter move into the guest room in my home. For two weeks, a pregnant young woman and her 72-year-old grandmother shared a pull-out sofa in a 200-square-foot guest room. What a huge step down from a 6,000-square-foot home, a home of promise and potential gone bad.

Physically, that young husband and NFL player removed every level of covering from his bride. He left her without his presence and shut off resources—resources vital to the well-being of his wife and unborn child.

I am thankful that my church and I were able to step in and provide the physical covering he refused to provide. Sadly, they divorced.

She requested nothing but child support. Today, she has recovered her life and her career. She's a loving, hard-working, and caring mother who refuses to let the ordeal make her bitter.

As for the athlete: His career ended abruptly. And he has yet to repent for what he did.

When Danger Lurks

As you can imagine, physical covering contributes profoundly to a woman's sense of security. When men are absent (or present in the wrong ways) covering is removed, and danger can creep in. I cannot count the numbers of women my wife and I have ministered to, over many years, who were molested as girls by uncles, cousins, neighbors, and even fathers and brothers. The stories are as plentiful as they are disturbing. I get sick to my stomach just thinking about them. The patterns in these stories are very consistent. Typically, the dad was either not in the home, emotionally disconnected from the home, or not in the female's life at all--unless he himself was the perpetrator.

The perpetrators were usually relatives or family friends who made themselves available to "help the family out." But their motives were anything but honorable.

It's mind-boggling to me how men leave the "gates" to their wives' and daughters' lives open and unprotected, allowing perverts to slip in unhindered. Men, it's our responsibility to protect our wives, our daughters, or any other girl or woman within our sphere of care. It's our job to make home a safe haven in a dangerous world. But a man who has abandoned ship or is rarely around is clueless about the dark elements trying to get in: shady neighbors, corrupt cousins, and so-called buddies with no boundaries, just to name a few. A man should keep a protective shield around his home and around his girls. He must be Mr. Security. He must be proactive. He should be man enough to call a spade a spade when he senses a foul spirit in another man. His message to such a man should be simple and straightforward: "Never come near my house, my wife, or my daughters."

I know a few people—including relatives, NFL players, and even a few church members—whom I wouldn't allow within 100 yards of my home. With a wife and three daughters (and a teenage son), I'm vigilant. For many years, I was considered the Weird Dad who wouldn't let his kids do sleepovers with schoolmates and relatives. But I didn't care what people thought.

Even my daughters were bothered by my tough stance. (I almost gave in to their pressure a couple of times.) But I could rest better knowing they were under my roof and in their beds, without strangers walking the halls at night. I understand that some dads mean well, but their lax standards give me pause. It isn't my business to tell them who should and should not be guests in their homes, but it is my business to monitor who is in *my* home. And it is my business to decide whose home I allow my girls to visit.

When She'd Really Rather Not . . .

Sometimes danger is not the issue. Sometimes covering is simply a matter of making life less stressful for a woman. A woman can do a lot of things if she feels she has no other choice. Many women can change a flat tire, take the car to the mechanic and drive a hard bargain, trim the hedges, or climb a ladder to clean out the rain gutters. But these duties can be stressful, physically dangerous, or both.

As I shared earlier, my dad didn't raise me. I didn't even meet him until years after I graduated from college.

So, when it was time for me to start college at Virginia Tech, my mother rented a van, packed up by belongings, and drove me from Norfolk to Blacksburg. She drove six hours through a mountainous region of the state that she'd never seen before. My mother never went to college, but she was determined that her "baby boy" would get there. She didn't let the lack of male covering in her life stop her. She did what had to be done.

For all my mother's strength--and the strength of countless other women-- there are some things that they'd rather not have to do. They do it because it must be done.

I applaud this courage and determination, but I contend that there are times when a man with a mind to cover can step in and make a huge difference and relieve significant burdens.

Sure, a woman can change that flat tire, but covering means she doesn't have to. A man committed to covering her makes sure he pays the annual AAA membership dues, or comes to the rescue himself.

That same woman might be quite capable of climbing the ladder to clean out the gutters. But how wonderful it is when the men of her church step up to cover her by doing the job themselves.

A man's physical presence can make life so much easier for the woman who has to "do it all on her own"--the single mother, the widow, or the wife whose husband is incapacitated. Given our physical strength, there are things we can do in half the time it might take her, especially when a group of men comes together to serve.

When Her Choices Are Unwise

One important expression of physical covering is needed when a woman's choices are unwise. I'm speaking particularly of our daughters. They can't always foresee the potential harm their choices can bring. A few years ago, when one of my daughters was just winding her way into puberty (and instant messaging was the rave), we had a bad scene at home. I'd told this daughter, firmly, several times, "No instant messaging for you. You are twelve years old, and there are sexual predators out there. So no instant messaging. End of discussion."

What do you think she did? You guessed it. I caught her IM'ing someone. She was having a conversation with a strange man. And, apparently, this was not the first conversation.

I'll spare you the details of my . . . OK, *explosion*. Let's just say I made some unilateral changes. This was not a time for diplomacy and debate with a 12-year-old. Neither was it a time to demand a false promise, such as, "I'll never, ever, do it again!"

I took her cell phone. (As in, took it and smashed it on the floor, while she looked on.) Drama queens need a little drama sometimes. That was a major blow to a girl whose social life by cell phone was *everything*.

But it didn't end there. Because my commitment is to covering her, I wanted to make sure she got the picture. If she wanted to live under my covering and my provision and have a relationship with everyone else in the family, trust was imperative. Because she'd broken the trust of the family, she had to repair that trust.

I called a family meeting. She explained her poor choice. I explained that I was just minutes away from escorting her to juvenile detention. Yes, juvenile detention.

I'll explain:

You see, if my daughter didn't want *my* protection and provision, she needed to consider another alternative for her life--perhaps somewhere she could live by her own rules. But she couldn't think of a place like that. So I called a police friend and had him arrange for a late-night trip to the Baltimore Juvenile Detention Center, located next door to the Baltimore City Jail. My daughter was horrified. Her siblings were awash with tears, and her grandmother pleaded with me by phone to re-consider. Her mother, on the other hand, knew this was a "scared straight" maneuver, and she supported me.

It worked. I took my 12-year-old to "juvy," where she was escorted by a very cooperative female officer to a cold-metal jail cell. All it had was a toilet, a sink, and a thinly covered slab of steel for a bed. It was a far cry from the comfortable home she was accustomed to. While she sat in the cell, out of my sight, I pretended to talk with the officer about how long they could keep her. An hour seemed to me like sufficient time for her to re-think her unwise choices. To my daughter, that hour felt like a lifetime.

My daughter changed almost instantly. Now we have a very special bond as father and daughter. She loves the fact that her daddy covers her—and she knows what that means. Sometimes, it means stepping in when she's headed in the wrong direction and giving her tough love. She's grown to be a committed follower of Christ, an honor student in her final undergraduate year, and has a servant's heart. She invites my counsel, and we deeply respect each other.

When Her Clothing Is Questionable

A final area in which so many of our girls need physical covering involves their clothing. Today's fashions for young women, in my humble opinion, have a lot to be desired. At the risk of sounding "Old School," I think it's unbecoming and unfortunate what the fashion industry pushes onto our young girls. Modesty has made a quick exit from our culture. Fashion seems to be about revealing as much flesh as possible. There's no mystery anymore, nothing left to the imagination.

My daughters aren't unaware of these fashion trends. So, as a dad who sees life and women from a man's perspective, it's important for me to wade into the clothing discussion with them. My girls all have different tastes, styles, and figures. They have their mom's beauty; they're all super-attractive. When it comes to what they wear, I do everything I can to celebrate their flare. I have them model their new jeans, sweaters, or ensembles. I even try to note their particular shoe tastes. But there are times when I have to say, "Oh, absolutely not! It's too open. It's too revealing. It attracts too much attention to that area of your body."

Sometimes they agree with me. Sometimes they vehemently disagree--and then the pressure is on:

"Dad, you don't understand the fashions today."

"Dad, you're Old School."

"Dad, *all* the girls at school wear these."

I'm telling you, it's tough, because it's hard to say no to those lovely ladies! But because I'm committed to cover them and encourage modesty, I have to be the bad guy sometimes.

It's astounding what some girls wear to school, and even to church. I want to ask them, "Did your dad see you leave the house? Does he really let you wear that? What kind of man do you think you'll attract, dressed as you are?"

As I travel around the country, speaking to men, I almost always bring up this topic. Though men are sometimes confounded and ashamed because they've displayed so little courage in this area, they are usually very grateful for some coaching on the topic.

Some are flat-out afraid to speak up, because they feel they have no authority. (Remember, authority comes from relationship, not from title.) Some have no authority because they don't have a connection with their daughters. Many simply don't know what to say. Others just don't care, because covering *costs*.

Covering costs time, energy, conversation, and money. If you're going to cover your girls from the wolves, you'd better start setting aside a clothing budget for them. When you're willing to "cough up the cheese," you gain credibility for the conversation. Ask your girls and your wife, "When was the last time you bought yourself a nice outfit?" Then slip them $50 or $100, if you can. If you can't, set aside ten bucks a week and when you have it all saved up, tell her, "I saved this just for you." And do it when it's not her birthday.

If you can, go to the mall with her and have lunch together. Her fashion choices will start to be influenced by your approval, not by cultural pressures.

Let me say a final word to all the dads who've been disconnected physically from your daughters because of failed relationships, failed marriages, and male selfishness. Guys, re-connect. She needs you, and it's not too late. Make the phone call. Mail the card. Tell her you're sorry for leaving her un-covered. Own your failure. Don't blame her mother. Don't blame the circumstances. Take responsibility. But whatever you do, do not come and go. Do not start, then stop again. Be consistent, even if it's a weekly phone call. Every girl wants a healthy connection to her daddy, even if she's 40 years old. Your words of earnest apology and affirmation can turn her self-concept right-side-up. Your renewed interest in her will remind her of her worth and that there's a princess inside of her.

Chapter 7 Instant Replay

1. A sense of being covered physically contributes profoundly to a woman's sense of security.

2. Sometimes, a man must step in when a daughter is making unsafe or unwise choices.

3. You earn your authority in a relationship from what you invest in that relationship—not from your title.

4. Every girl wants a healthy connection to her daddy—even if she's 40 years old.

When A Woman
Needs You Emotionally
(Emotional Covering)

8

You don't have to be a football superstar or a genius to be a great coach. Some really good NFL coaches never played pro ball. And many of them were willing to work their way up the ranks as they learned the game. Ravens Head Coach John Harbaugh, my dear friend, did not play in the NFL like his younger brother, Jim. After his college playing career, John helped his father as graduate-assistant coach at Western Michigan. He eventually found a job as a special-teams coordinator at Indiana University. He worked his way up the college coaching ranks, but when he moved to the NFL, he started near the bottom of the ladder again, working as special-teams coordinator for the Philadelphia Eagles.

Effective coaches like John have *learned* their craft over time. They know how to stand outside a situation, observe, give input, and then inspire a player to maximize his or her potential. I'm no expert on the emotional makeup and needs of women, but I've learned some things from years of observation, experience, and personal fumbles.

What I've learned, I'd like to pass on to you. To use an NFL term, I'd like to "coach you up" on emotional covering by giving you five important tips. Some of what I challenge you to do will be tough, uncomfortable, and awkward. It will stretch you, but you will get better and you will win in a big way!

Emotionally weak men who cave easily under pressure can't cover a woman. If that's you, you will need to make up your mind to be a pillar of strength rather than be a man whose feelings are easily hurt and who's still looking for his mother's affection. Real men do cry. But for now, you will need to find somewhere else to shed your tears. A woman needs your inner emotional strength.

Now is not the time for the men who look strong on the outside— with gruff voices, tattoos, and bulging biceps--but who can't handle the emotional needs of a daughter whose hormones are raging or who struggles with her self-worth. Now is the time to "be strong, show yourself a man, and observe what the LORD your God requires." (1 Kings 2:2-3a) A man who can build up a woman emotionally, with pure motives, is a powerful man!

Too many of us check out of the emotional dialogue with women when we're most needed. But it's time we learn to tune in and pour in, emotionally. Whether it's our wives, our daughters, our sisters, or our female friends who need an emotional boost, we have what it takes to support them. But we must be careful not to cross lines into inappropriate conversation, touch, or emotional entanglement. Our motives must be pure and our hearts must be clean before God, otherwise we'll make a big emotional mess. Our prayer, before extending emotional covering should be the same as King David's: "Create in me a clean heart, O God; and renew a right spirit within me." (Psalms 51:10 KJV)

The man who can make healthy emotional investments will become a hero and be known as a strong man--a difference maker.

Coaching Tip #1: Respect the Reality of Hormones

When a man says a woman is "hormonal," he means that her hormones are driving her words and actions. The truth is that we are *all* hormonal to some degree. All our bodies produce testosterone, estrogen, and progesterone (three hormones you may be familiar with). Our differences lie in our hormone levels. A man's body produces much higher levels of testosterone, while a woman's body produces much higher levels of estrogen. Testosterone is commonly known as the "male hormone," while estrogen is known as the "female hormone." The levels of any key hormones can influence how we feel and function--on many different levels. They affect energy levels, libido, mood, sleep habits, self-confidence, and even food cravings.

OK, enough about hormones. You don't have to be an expert on the subject to provide effective covering. However, you must respect the fact that hormones have a very real impact on you, your daughters, your wife, and every other woman you know. There's no getting around the biology that affects emotions and moods.

Because you and I are called to cover, it only makes sense that we assume that hormones *may be* a factor. There are certain times of the month that a woman or teen might feel tired or clingy or self-conscious about her appearance. She may have a lot to say and be particularly outgoing on the days when her estrogen levels are

On her website myhormonesmademedoit.com, Gabrielle Lichterman does a great job discussing the hormone cycles women experience throughout the month, as well as a man's 24-hour hormone cycle.

high. On other days, she may be down and irritable because her estrogen levels have hit bottom. Do not take this personally. You must learn how to flow with it, instead of against it. Cover her by accommodating her. Ask questions like these:

"Can I do anything for you?"

"Do you need some time alone?"

"Would you like me to sit here and cuddle with you?"

"I'll be happy to bring you home some chocolate when I leave work—would you like that?"

"I'm sorry you feel so poorly today. How can I help?"

The apostle Peter said it best: "Husbands, in the same way be considerate as you live with your wives, and treat them with respect as the weaker partner and as heirs with you of the gracious gift of life, so that nothing will hinder your prayers." (1 Peter 3:7)

Whether she's your wife, your daughter, or your sister, the same principles apply. Treat them with respect, not with condescension, when their hormones are doing what they do. Weaker doesn't mean lesser; it simply means weaker than a man. She doesn't have a man's physical strength, and she handles her hormones' effect on her differently than a man does.

Coaching Tip #2: Tell Her How Valuable She Is

When my wife and I were struggling missionaries, living in Los Angeles with four small children, we often wondered how we would survive financially. We wondered if we should look for different work. It became apparent to me that whenever money got tight, my wife would talk about the career she could have had in medicine. She wondered if she had squandered away her life in ministry, because many of our peers were well along in their business and medical careers.

But I didn't want her having to wake at 5 every morning--not to nurse our youngest baby--but to take three buses across town to work in a medical building. We would have had to put all of our children in daycare. That wasn't an option for me.

After a while, I realized that Sheri's fear of finances was a secondary issue. The real issue was a struggle with her sense of self-worth. Smelly diapers, mountains of laundry, an unending cycle of dishes in the sink, and living pay-check-to-paycheck don't say a lot to a woman about her value, especially when she graduated Summa Cum Laude with a double major in biology and zoology. So I began to tell her how much she was worth to me and to our young family. I insisted that she have a weekly day off from mommy duties. We started going on weekly dates, and I arranged for the childcare. I began to thank her for making sure I had clean underwear every day and for keeping our home so comfortable. I reminded her that my work was *nothing* without her sacrifice.

You know what happened? She took her entire mommy-wife game to a new level--new recipes, new day ventures for the kids, and fewer complaints about my work schedule. The money didn't improve significantly, but my wife began to feel more valuable in her duties.

I learned a priceless lesson from our years in Los Angeles: Always remind Sheri and the girls of how valuable they are.

Men, tell the ladies, "I'm so glad you are in my life!" They often think your work is more important and that they are getting in the way of our "real love": the career. Remind them of how their unique personalities add so much to life at home. Let them know that life wouldn't be the same without them. I tell my wife she means so much to me that if she dies, it's going to be a 2-for-1 burial, because I'm getting in the casket with her. She knows I'm kidding, but she gets the point. I don't want to have to live without her.

Coaching Tip #3: Tell Her, Often, How Beautiful She Is

Women never get tired of hearing they're beautiful. When my daughters were little girls, they had a chest called the dress-up box. Hour after hour, they would put on wigs, dresses, and shoes passed down from my wife and other women. Oh, what a sight! It was the funniest thing to watch them parade and sashay across the room in women's clothes three times too large. They'd say, in their made-up British accents, "Father, how do I look?"

> *Tell your wife, "I'm so glad you are in my life!" She might think your work is more important and that she is getting in the way of your "real love": the career.*

The answer was the same as it is today: "Ooooweee, baby girl, you look beautiful! Like a million bucks!"

As long as they could find clothes in the box, and as long as I had time to be the judge of the beauty contest, they'd continue.

Nothing has changed with the passing of years. At ages 16, 19, and 21, they still like to hear me say how beautiful they look. Whether they're getting dressed for a formal engagement or for a movie with friends, they still come by my study, waiting for my words: "You look beautiful!"

It never gets old to them or to their mother, my bride. Sometimes, I don't even address them by name. I just say, "Hey, beautiful, how's your day going?" --whether by text message or in person. They love it.

Just yesterday, my wife called me on my cell phone while I was in my study writing. She'd gone out to drop off the dry-cleaning. As she was getting out of her car, she noticed she had caught a gentleman's eye. She turned away, only to see him looking again. She was unsure if she knew him.

Eventually, he said, "Good morning."

Sheri, being polite, replied, "Good morning. How are you?"

He stumbled all over himself, saying what he couldn't help but express: "You are really pretty!"

That's why my wife called me—to report that a strange man was flirting with her. But I was not threatened. I responded, "I'm not mad at him. He's absolutely right. The next time you're in a situation like that, tell him your husband said he's right. And then let him know that you're not thirsty for compliments because your husband tells you every day how beautiful you are to him! And if he has anything else to say, call me and I'll come deal with him."

Men, so many of the girls in our churches and communities are growing up emotionally starved for male affection. Don't let your daughters and your wives leave home thirsty for those soul-filling affirmations of their beauty. Otherwise, the first person who comes along and begins to fill their emotional love tanks may capture their affections and their imaginations--even if he's a bum.

I know what you're thinking, men. Sometimes the ladies don't look their best. In the morning when the hair is all messed up, and the makeup is off, what can we say without lying? That's when you have to be man enough to see beyond the outside appearance. Tell them they're beautiful because you see it on the inside. When you do, she will take care of business on the outside.

Maybe you didn't know this, but God has given you a powerful voice to help her become what He has designed her to be. When Adam first saw Eve, he declared what she was: "She shall be called Woman." (Genesis 2:23 KJV) God gave Adam the privilege and the authority to name her. In like manner, Jesus loved and sacrificed His life for a church, which had not yet come into existence. He died, believing in what she would someday be: a bride that is holy (special), pure, radiant, spotless, blameless, and blemish-free. (See Ephesians 5:26-27.) Men, whatever you want her to be, you must declare with words of affirmation and blessing! Declare her beautiful and watch her become it.

Coaching Tip #4: Guide Her Gently If She's Uncertain Which Way to Go

Decisions are tough to make, no matter who you are. But when decisions involve major life issues, a woman can feel overwhelmed. What should she do about a good friend who deeply wounded her? Where should she go to college? How should she respond to painful changes in a life-long friendship? Should she date the young man who's interested in her? Should she choose business or music as her major in college?

Life can begin to feel very uncertain. And when it does, it's helpful to have emotional covering that gently guides a woman to the shoreline of clarity.

A dad or a husband or a respected leader in the church can be an invaluable sounding board during times of crisis and fog. A listening and wise ear helps to remove the feelings of danger and impending destruction from those life-changing decisions. It's an amazing honor to have teen girls in my church schedule appointments with me, their pastor, to seek counsel about tough decisions they're dealing with. I try to guide them as if they were my own daughters. Usually, questions are more helpful than instructions, enabling them to form healthy long-term conclusions.

I ask,

"What's most important to you?"

"What Scriptures have been speaking to you, lately?"

"Is there an issue of sin that could hinder you from hearing God's voice?"

"What are some of your goals? Have you written them on paper?"

"Which of your options most closely aligns with your written goals?"

"Can you list the possible consequences that might follow this decision?"

"Is the young man you're interested in committed to growing in his relationship with Christ and serving in his local church?"

Let me add the severest word of warning here. It's one thing to guide your wife or your own daughters. It's quite another thing to guide girls or a woman who aren't yours. Never, ever, do it in isolation, behind closed doors, and without the open communication of a small team. Too many girls and young women have been preyed upon by wolves in sheep's clothing, inside and outside the church.

Never offer guidance or counsel without both the presence and the permission of parents when a minor is involved. A parent's presence or that of a youth staff worker, for example, provides safety for all involved. Do not text or email girls who aren't your children. In the same vein, limit telephone, text, and email contact with women who are not your wife.

Finally, beware of the Superman Syndrome. It's not your job to rescue every female in distress. A great way to guide is to point women to *other women* who can be a resource to them. If your boundaries are not clear and appropriate, you could cause irreparable emotional damage, all in the name of emotional covering.

Chapter 8 Instant Replay

1. Emotionally weak men who cave under pressure cannot cover a woman.

2. The truly powerful man is the guy who can build up a woman emotionally and spiritually.

3. Beware of the Superman Syndrome. It's not your job to rescue every female in distress.

4. Be very cautious about providing emotional covering to women or girls outside your family.

When A Woman Needs You Spiritually (Spiritual Covering)

9

The most selfless and most valuable thing a man can offer a woman is neither sex nor money. (Sorry to disappoint you, brothers.) It's biblical spiritual direction and support. But too many men look to their wives and mothers to lead the way spiritually. We're busy watching the football game rather than building our spiritual muscles. When the script is flipped and men actually become the ones pointing the way with prayer, Scripture, and faith, women readily and joyfully take their God-ordained place as the family nurturer. Their respect level for their man rises. Because he's a man with "spiritual game," he doesn't have to be the best-looking guy in the building. His poise and his swagger, when spiritually rooted in the dynamic and faithful God of the Bible, make him more attractive than Denzel Washington and Tom Cruise combined. And if he knows how to connect his authentic masculine faith to a woman's spiritual needs, he becomes the man she can't stop talking about!

Whether you're a single young man in his 20s or you've been married for 30 years, this chapter is one you should read thoroughly and thoughtfully. Too many men have surrendered spiritual leadership to their mothers, aunties, and wives. We've thrown out the baby with the bath water, assuming the Christian faith is too effeminate for the no-nonsense CEO, the competitive athlete, or even the weekend warrior. I know: Churches and worship services seem to be designed for their majority-female congregations. But don't take your cues from that. Spiritual leadership is for masculine men. It's time we marry the relentless courage of Joshua with the passionate worship of David to produce a generation of men who will take back the family and the community for God!

When She's Been Overwhelmed

King David made one of the worst mistakes of his life when he fled to a place called Ziklag. (See the story in 1 Samuel, chapters 27, 29, and 30.) David had been anointed by the judge/prophet Samuel, but he had yet to take his seat on Israel's thrown. The promise spoken over his life (in 1 Samuel 16) seemed like a distant figment of his imagination as he spent nearly 15 years running from his predecessor, King Saul, a man whom he had served faithfully. For all those years, the man David had called "my lord" was consumed with wiping him from the face of the earth. Saul considered the young man a threat to his popularity and his power. Understandably, David grew weary and discouraged. He decided he'd be better off hiding out in the hometown of his defeated enemy, Goliath, and feigning mental illness, than dealing with Saul. He even aligned himself with Achish, king of the Philistines, David's archenemies. This should make us ask, "Why would anyone man make himself a subject in the territory of an enemy he's already defeated?"

Like many of us, David was simply worn down by fighting for survival at every turn. After all, how many spears can one man dodge? How many nights can one hide in a cave? David figured if he had to fight for his life all the time, he might as well join his enemies.

While he was searching for relief from the pressure, David found himself disconnected from God. During the 18 months he spent at Ziklag, David didn't pen a single Psalm. The pressures of life had pushed him far away from the habits of worship and prayer he was once known for. This anointed "man after God's own heart" lost connection with his God.

Many of us are exactly where David was. Life has worn us down, and we've lost our "umph" for God.

But God knows just what we need to revive our spiritual passions and our spiritual courage. David and his men eventually left camp Ziklag, only to return later and find that their tents had been burned down and their women and children taken by the Amalekites. The people David and his men were responsible for covering were now in the enemy's hands. David's men talked of stoning him. They were understandably furious. The man who was supposed to be their spiritual and tactical leader had led them to familial, emotional, and moral disaster. God had allowed their women and children to be overwhelmed by their enemies.

This grave situation served a deeply beneficial purpose in David's life. It caused him to turn back to the God who had announced a prophetic promise to make him king. The women and children under David's covering didn't stand a chance of surviving if David did not reconnect with the Source of his strength. David called for

Abiathar the priest to bring out the linen ephod, by which he could inquire of God--something David had not done in 18 months. For all that time, David had been making decisions without the counsel of the Wonderful Counselor!

His neglect of God got him and everyone connected to him in serious trouble. But David sought the Lord again, and God heard his desperate cry for help. First Samuel 30:18 sums up the outcome of David's drama: "David recovered everything the Amalekites had taken, including his two wives." But he had to fight like crazy.

Men, our connection to God is utterly important. Without it, the spiritual covering God provides through us can be removed from our wives and children and others who depend on our spiritual leadership. They can be overwhelmed by the enemy. The only way to help them is by re-connecting with the

> *So much is riding on your relationship with God! Your wife and your children can't fight the enemy you were designed to protect them from. You are their spiritual covering.*
> *No one else can fill this role like you can.*

Almighty. I know the pressure you're dealing with is draining, and it might feel like a better option to align with the enemy. These options include an adulterous affair, divorce, internet pornography, an addictive substance, or even a life of leisure.

There are times when such pursuits seem more attractive than worshiping in God's house. But there's too much riding on your relationship with God. Your wife and your children can't fight the enemy you were designed to protect them from. You are their spiritual covering. No one else can fill this role like you can.

When Her Guard Is Down

Just as David's wives and children and those of his men didn't see the Amalekites coming to subdue them, Eve had no idea that the serpent she was talking with was trying to undermine God's purposes for humanity. She had no idea he would use her as a pawn in his chess match with God, whom he hated. Eve let her spiritual guard down. I don't know why she thought she could entertain someone who questioned God's truth without creating huge problems.

But Eve is really not the one I'm miffed at in the Garden story. My issue is with Adam, the one to whom God gave the command not to eat from the tree in the middle of the Garden. It was Adam's responsibility to relay this command to his woman. It was his duty to press the issue of obedience when she entertained suspicions of God's good motives. (When the serpent told her, "For God knows that when you eat of it your eyes will be opened, and you will be like God, knowing good and evil.")

Why did Eve let her guard down with the serpent? Maybe she thought he meant no harm. He just wanted to chat. Maybe she didn't want to seem rude to someone who was kind enough to engage her intellectually and philosophically.

Women can be very unsuspecting and overly kind. And it's just not wise. So often, I've watched couples fight over destructive decisions, and the wife will say something like, "He seemed like such a nice man. I didn't think he'd do that to me. He seemed harmless."

One wife I know allowed her husband's "friend" to talk her into loaning him $100,000--without telling her husband. Yes, you read the figure right: $100,000. He convinced her that he really needed the money, that his life was in danger, and that he'd return the money before her husband would ever miss it from their savings account. But after calling, begging, and pleading with the swindler, the money never came. When the husband found out, it nearly destroyed their marriage. How could he ever trust the woman he once trusted with his life? After several months and a messy battle, they got the money back, but at a severe cost to their relationship. Broken trust takes a long time to re-build.

What happened with the couple above is not very different from what happened with Adam and Eve. Like fumbling a hot potato in his hand, Adam dropped his opportunity to cover Eve when her guard was down. As we saw earlier in the book, Eve "also gave [fruit] to her husband with her, and he ate it." (Genesis 3:6 NKJV)

Rather than speak up, Adam stood by in silence. Then he participated in the disobedience, without question. Perhaps he was perplexed, but he had no excuse. Most theologians suggest Adam was present when Eve was tempted, yet he looked on in passive silence.

I, too, believe that Adam was there, right next to Eve. But like so many men, he wasn't really *all* there. In other words, maybe Adam didn't pay attention until it was too late. Like the husband in the story above, Adam might have been too busy with his work to notice that Eve didn't have her spiritual guard in place. After all, how else did they drift so close to that forbidden tree in the first place?

Why wasn't Adam paying attention to Eve's conversation? Eve was having a meaningful dialogue, and it *wasn't* with her husband.

Men, spiritual covering means paying attention to the daily patterns of our wives and daughters. Have they stopped enjoying listening to the preached Word and praise music in the car? Has their conversation changed? Have their friends changed? Have their attitudes shifted? Has their dress style changed drastically—without any input from you? Is there an unusual look in their eyes?

Has your wife lost her libido? Is she spending more money than normal? Their guards may be down, and they might not even realize it. But it's on *us* to speak to the subtle changes we see and to remind them of God's words, such as, "Don't be unequally yoked" and "Bad company corrupts good morals."

Tell her if her new girlfriends are hindering her walk with God. Ask her what she's been reading in her private devotions with God--and join her. Are you washing her with the Word, leading her to worship, and bathing her daily in prayer?

We can't afford to sit by idly or to be consumed with our work. We have to be watchful and speak up, because the consequences could be generational. Sure, she may think you're holier-than-thou, especially if your approach is not spiritually sensitive. But someday she'll thank you for having the courage to speak up.

When You Can't Be There

My work as a pastor, chaplain, and speaker means I log a lot of miles in the friendly skies. Weekend trips for ministry with an NFL team are anything but glamorous sometimes, especially when they are cross-country and we return home at 4 o'clock on a Monday morning. For 14 NFL seasons, the hardest part about traveling has been missing my wife and kids. But the years have also been very rewarding, spiritually. Sheri has been gracious and extremely supportive. She and the kids always look for me on the sidelines on television. They know there are times when, because of my commitment to my calling, I just can't be home. But just because I can't be home, doesn't mean I can't still cover my family spiritually.

Prayer is a power and effective weapon for followers of Jesus. Men with demanding travel schedules or who have long work days in town can still cover our wives and children with prayer. We can be anywhere in the world, at any time of day, and commune with God in prayer. Whether I'm in a hotel room in San Diego or standing on the sidelines before a game in the Georgia Dome, I can lift up prayers for my wife and kids. Prayer allows me to speak into the invisible realm to an invisible God who is more real than the air I breathe. Even though we can't see Him, He acts with power and precision in the lives of those we cover.

When my wife's day is filled with drama and I'm not there, I call her on the phone and we pray together. This calms her. It reminds her that she's covered and that God cares. When my daughters are weighed down with exams, nervous about performances, or facing tough decisions, their daddy's prayers tell them that God is on their side. They begin to sense victory, and they feel a great sense of relief.

For some men, this might seem like a stretch, but you don't have to be a spiritual giant to cover her this way. Shoot her a text: "I'm praying for you today." Text-message the prayer itself: "Father, give her victory at work today, in Jesus' name."

When you read a verse of Scripture that will encourage her, email it to her or tweet it to her. Whatever you do, my friend, stay connected spiritually when you can't be their physically. You will communicate that you are still connected and that you fully support her.

When She's Not Quite a Woman Yet

Men, why do so many of us readily turn our daughters over to the care of other men—guys we don't really know? Why can some stranger just walk into a girl's life, without having to meet some reasonable standards? Why trust a young guy with a daughter's emotional and physical well-being—when his only major accomplishment is surviving puberty?

Given all I've invested in my daughters since their births, I refuse to allow some knuckle-head to come in and sweep them off their feet. Because I've paid the emotional cost, invested the relationship capital, and have spent good money to prepare them for life, the young man who wants to date my girls must come through me. I make no bones about it: He cannot pursue her without having to put forth an earnest effort to prove he values them as much as I do.

Consider Jacob of the Old Testament. He fell in love with Rachel, the younger daughter of his Uncle Laban, and he was willing to put in work to have her. He worked seven years for the privilege. Most men in our modern culture won't work seven days for the honor of having a woman. It's an entitled and impatient generation. But not Jacob. He made his intentions clear. He was committed to the process, and he valued Rachel highly! Any man who will work seven years for a woman sees something valuable in her.

Yet, we give our daughters over to complete strangers because they "seem like nice guys." What's wrong with us? Love must prove itself.

Men, we could spare our daughters and our families serious headaches if we'd be strong enough to set the bar high. After all, who has the time for years of casual, non-committal dating? Don't let your daughter cheapen herself, and don't *you* cheapen her. She's more valuable than that. She deserves high standards. That is part of your spiritual covering for her. This means tossing out all the culturally acceptable approaches to dating that you grew up with-- and the "hanging out" code her peers operate by.

There would be no hanging out for Jacob. That brother had to work for the woman he wanted.

What's even more impressive than Jacob's willingness to work seven years to get Rachel is his willingness to work seven *more* years after he'd been tricked by Laban. One morning, Jacob woke to find himself lying naked next to Rachel's sister, Leah, instead of Rachel. Laban had pulled a switcheroo on him in the middle of the night! What do you do when the woman you wake up with is the sister of the one you worked seven years for? How do you face the disappointment?

Jacob endured the disappointment and the unfair treatment, because his heart was set on Rachel. He agreed to work seven more years, after the fact, if he got Rachel as his bride. Jacob got a raw deal, but he worked as hard after he got Rachel as he did before.

Men, we can learn a lesson from this saga. Watch how the young man who wants to date your daughter deals with the disappointment of not getting what he wants. Observe whether he is committed and patient enough to wait it out and to work it out. How far is he willing to drive? How hard is he willing to work for the relationship? How much money is he willing to invest for her hand? How much is he willing to be stretched?

As spiritual covering for our maturing young women, we have to teach them that standards matter. We have to let them know that we value them so much that we refuse to hand them over to a good-looking fast-talker with no vision, no patience, and no work ethic.

I approach it this way: If a young man is unwilling to deal humbly and directly with me, he won't have access to my daughters. This is a rule established for their protection.

Dads, our daughters should be able to count on our watchful presence when it comes to suitors. Let them know the bar has been set high because you want to give them away, on their wedding day, to the right man: the man who has proven himself over time to be committed to doing whatever it takes to demonstrate his love.

Chapter 9 Instant Replay

1. The most valuable thing a man can offer a woman is biblically based direction and support.

2. Too many men have fumbled their responsibility to be spiritual leaders in their homes.

3. Men, spiritual covering means paying attention to the *daily patterns* of our wives and daughters

4. If you're a dad, potential suitors should have to deal humbly and directly with you if they want to date your daughter.

CHAPTER 10
Live-In-Lover, But No Cover

10

Our modern culture is one of live-in lovers. So often, men and women choose to live together without being married--and *instead* of getting married. What was once frowned upon is now widely accepted. Fewer and fewer parents discourage the practice for their sons and daughters, naively assuming they're moving toward marriage.

Usually, this is an arrangement of logic and convenience rather than one of sacrifice and commitment. The rationale goes something like this: "We love each other, so we might as well save some money and combine our households."

All the so-called benefits of the arrangement are immediate. There are absolutely no guarantees for the future.

In my many years of ministry to athletes, I've realized that there's a familiar theme to the live-in arrangement: the man's sexual pleasure. I've seen this movie over and over: A player arrives in the NFL. He makes the roster, and soon settles into an apartment with a girlfriend.

As the player and I get to know each other, I ask the inevitable question: "Are you planning to marry her soon?"

The answers range from, "I'm not ready for that yet, Rev!" to "Maybe in a few years, when I'm financially secure."

It's very rare, by the way, to find a player who lives with a girlfriend but abstains from sex—even in college football.

When I ask players about their commitment to their girlfriends, the reply is usually, "Yeah, we're committed." Some of them even call a girlfriend "wifey" or "the wife." In their minds, living together is the equivalent of marriage. That's why I remind them that they're playing house like children. If there is no marriage certificate, there's no marriage. They usually just chuckle and keep doing what they're doing.

In these relationships, the guy usually expects the girl to be monogamous. But, between you and me, he doesn't hold himself to the same standard.

Often, a player expects his girlfriend to get a job and contribute to the "household" income. Meanwhile, she doesn't have access to his bank account, and she's not on his medical insurance, unless she gets pregnant. She's usually not the beneficiary on his life insurance policy. So, if the player loses his job, squanders his money, or dies, his girl is left with virtually nothing, except, perhaps, child support.

What kind of man will make a woman his live-in "concubine" and not give her guaranteed legal coverage as his wife? What kind of father allows his daughter to waltz naively into a living arrangement with a man who won't cover her? Sadly, this type of man represents a rapidly expanding element of male leadership in our culture.

In the Bible, living together before marriage was unthinkable. Responsibility was woven into the fabric of family life. The standard for men was clear: When a woman becomes your wife, her care becomes your responsibility, not her daddy's. Once you take her home, you dishonor her if she has to go back to her parents.

> *In the Bible, living together before marriage was unthinkable. Responsibility was woven into the fabric of family life. The standard for men was clear: When a woman becomes your wife, her care becomes your responsibility, not her daddy's.*

With this background in mind, let's look at the weakness of the live-in lover arrangement and how it robs a woman's security, rather than builds it. The truth of the matter is that men who play the live-in lover game want all the benefits of committed love without the risk and commitment that this love demands of them.

We have to demand more of ourselves, more of our sons, and more of those who desire the companionship of the daughters we cover. Refuse to endorse modern concubinage and call younger men to a higher standard of leadership.

If your daughters insist on being "concubines," you have no other option but to pray for them and to let them know the expense of the wedding, if there ever is one, is on them. At the same time, remind them what treasures they are. Tell that daughter, "You're worth more than being someone's convenient living partner."

Chapter 10 Instant Replay

1. The modern live-in-lover arrangement weakens a woman's sense of security, rather than building it.

2. We need to tell our daughters, "You're worth more than being someone's convenient living partner."

3. If there's no marriage certificate, there's no marriage.

CHAPTER 11
Role Models:
How the Players Cover

11

During my years of ministry in the NFL, I have built relationships with many strong and godly men—men who are committed to their families. In this chapter, I have asked a few of these men to share their thoughts on family and faith, and to describe how they keep their families covered.

Bernard Pollard currently plays safety for the Tennessee Titans. Last season, he was named to *USA Today's* All-Joe Team, which honors top-flight players who do not get the acclaim they deserve.

His hard-hitting style of play earned him the nickname "The Bonecrusher" in college. He was a member of the Ravens recent Super Bowl championship team, playing almost the entire season with painful rib injuries.

"Sometimes I see other players get so wrapped up in their careers and the life of a pro athlete that they get lost. In the NFL, you're away from home at least eight times during the season—more if you make the playoffs. With all that time away, and the temptations that come with it, people fall. It just hits them out of the blue.

"For me, I see what I stand to lose. I have been married more than five years, and I have three beautiful kids. I simply cannot make those mistakes—the ones I've seen other players make. It helps me to stay in the Scriptures, and to think about men like Samson. He was blessed with so much, but he did the one thing God warned him *not* to do.

"As a professional athlete, you have to take your attention *home*. My wife and I have consistent dialogue between us, and I stay in constant communication with my kids.

"Lately, I am encouraged to see more NFL players wanting that strong relationship with their wives or significant others. They want to do right by them."

Billy Bajema plays tight end for the World Champion Baltimore Ravens. Billy is a versatile athlete who, in high school, played both quarterback and defensive end.

"Men are the same inside and outside of football. The culture presents similar challenges to all of us. As a relatively young husband and father, I want to make my family a priority. I want to raise my kids to know and serve the Lord.

"God gave me the ability to play football, and I want to make the most of it. Colossians 3:23 says, 'And whatever you do, do it heartily, as to the Lord and not to men.' I think about that verse a lot, including when I'm about to take the field.

"As a Christian, I have found that other players respect where I'm coming from—and what I stand for. They see that I don't go out to the clubs and things like that. They see I have a strong faith, and they respect that. My faith creates conversations with other players, and I've had the opportunity to invite guys to chapel services."

Matt Birk recently retired after 15 years in the NFL. He was a six-time Pro Bowl center, as well as the league's 2011 Walter Payton Man of the Year, which recognizes excellence on and off the field. Matt graduated from Harvard. Ravens teammate Michael Oher called him "the best leader ever."

"As an NFL player, taking care of business on the field was about the 10th most important thing in my life. To me, it was more important to love my wife and to be the shepherd of my six kids' hearts. You have to make the effort daily. When you're home, be *home*. Don't be distracted. Emails and things like that can wait. Give your family your time; it's the most valuable thing you can give. I've never heard of anybody regretting the time he spent with his family. And remember, you're only as happy as your saddest child.

> *"As an NFL player, taking care of business on the field was about the 10th most important thing in my life. To me, it was more important to love my wife and to be the shepherd of my six kids' hearts."*
> *Matt Birk*

"Prayer is so important to me. Sometimes, I will lie there on the floor in one of the kids' rooms, and I'll pray, 'Help me, God. I'm getting' my butt kicked.' I pray all the time for energy and fortitude and wisdom.

"In football and in life, all God wants is my best. Win or lose, you need God in both cases."

Anquan Boldin is a veteran wide receiver for the San Francisco 49ers. He is a three-time Pro Bowler, and in 2003 he was named NFL Offensive Rookie of the Year. The 2013 season marks his 11th year in the NFL. As this book went to press, he led the league in receiving yardage.

"In the NFL arena, there's a lot of 'It's all about me.' A lot of players have been catered to their entire lives, because they've been dominant athletes, even at an early age. But when you get married and have a family, it's no longer about 'Me.' You have to make sacrifices for your wife. You have to treat her like she's your queen. You have to be unselfish.

"I know my two sons are watching me, and if I am disrespectful to my wife, they'll take note. I have to bite my tongue a lot! I want to live out the Word of God and give of myself. Life is not about winning football games; it's about a greater good. It's about Kingdom business."

Ben Grubbs is a Pro Bowl guard for the New Orleans Saints. The seven-year veteran is one of the most athletic linemen in the NFL. He has close to 5.0-second speed in the 40-yard-dash. In high school, he starred in basketball as well as football—where he was a linebacker on defense and a fullback on offense.

"This season (2013-2014) is my first one as a married player. Training camp was a tough time. It's really hard to get face-time with your wife during the three to four weeks of camp. But you do your best to have open lines of communication. Technology is great for that. And during challenging times, I strive to consider her feelings. I remind myself that things are tough for her too, not just for me.

"As a new husband, I ask myself all the time: 'How can I serve my wife?' That's something Pastor Rod taught me. He helped me understand that to be a leader, you first have to serve.

"Pastor Rod is one of several strong male role models I've had in my life. My dad died when I was five years old, so I grew up in a single-parent home. There was an empty space that needed to be filled. But God provided someone at every level: My head coach in high school. The chaplain at Auburn University—he was a great guy and chaplain. He made sure our souls were spiritually filled. He was one of the reasons we were so successful at Auburn.

"Another guy is Matt Birk, a teammate when I played for the Ravens. He is a great man, on and off the field. He led by example. He would invite us linemen to his house. Seeing how much he loves his wife and his six kids, how much attention he gave them, that spoke volumes to me."

Rod Woodson is one of the greatest defensive backs to ever play the game. He is an NFL Hall of Famer who was also selected to the league's 75th Anniversary Team. Rod made the Pro Bowl 11 times, and he was Defensive Player of the Year in 1993. He played for 17 seasons and retired as pro football's all-time leader in interception-return yardage. Rod was also a world-class track athlete. He was always one of the fastest players in the NFL.

"Men's troubles with being good husbands and fathers haven't changed much during my many years in the NFL. The troubles go back way beyond football. Some men are not living up to their duties.

"For me, where you are at in your spiritual life makes all the difference. I have had great men of God in my life. They've shown me how to live the right way. Men like Napoleon Kauffman and Rod Hairston have told me, 'Don't hang up on God. Don't you hang up on Him.'

"Also, I make verses like 1 John 2:6 part of my day-to-day walk: 'Whoever claims to live in him must live as Jesus did.'

"At home, I don't want to say that God is a big part of my life, and then be a hypocrite. I don't want to be that kind of person to my children—to tell them one thing, then do another.

"I have a 23-year-old daughter, and I am telling her to take it slow in her dating life. I want her to listen to Christ. As for the guy she's dating, I want him to fear God. I want him to love his family and show compassion on a day-in and day-out basis. And he should serve in his church in some capacity."

Chapter 11 Instant Replay

1. "As a new husband, I ask myself all the time: 'How can I serve my wife?'"—Ben Grubbs

2. "Give your family your time; it's the most valuable thing you can give. I've never heard of anybody regretting the time he spent with his family."—Matt Birk

3. "You have to make sacrifices for your wife. You have to treat her like she's your queen. You have to be unselfish."--Anquan Boldin

CHAPTER 12
Looking Her Pain In The Eyes
(Un-Covered Daughters, Fragile Women)

12

When couples come to me for marriage counseling or invite me to their weddings, I ask them, "Which of your partner's *weaknesses* are you most excited about living with for the rest of your life?" They are understandably taken aback. Most people don't consider all of the weaknesses, idiosyncrasies, and unresolved issues they will be taking on when they say, "I do."

I once heard Bishop T.D. Jakes say, "We are attracted to each other's strengths, but we marry one another's weaknesses." That wisdom stuck with me, and I try to help couples think about its truth.

If they can honestly wrestle with this issue, they have a really good chance at succeeding in marriage.

When a man proposes to a woman, he's excited about his "amazing catch" of a lifelong mate. But even amazing people bring faults to a marriage. Every marriage is a perfect storm of imperfections, brokenness, and pain in each spouse. Men who choose to cover courageously aren't afraid to look a woman's pain in the eye. They refuse to wander away from her.

A strong man is unafraid of the challenging things he learns about his wife's past. In this chapter, I want to help men tackle the painful issues that women bring into their marriages—often because they were uncovered as daughters.

Many women enter marriage with histories of sexual, physical, or emotional abuse, as well as neglect, abandonment, or other hurts that they've never resolved. I've talked with women who were molested by fathers and brothers, but they didn't tell their husbands about it, even after 10 or 20 years of marriage.

I've counseled other women whose pastors had taken advantage of them sexually. Still others were abandoned by their fathers and lied to constantly. Some were in abusive relationships throughout their teenage and young adult lives. And now these women are in marriages or closing in on their wedding day.

In many instances, they've developed survival skills and coping mechanisms that seem, understandably, normal to them. But obsessive calorie counting, compulsive exercise regimens, or serial sex partners--often from a young age--are anything but normal.

These women didn't really want to hide who they were and what they had experienced, but that's what they had to do to survive. Some of them resolved never to mention what happened, hoping they could move forward in life and find "normalcy." They called a tragedy "just a thing that happened."

By the grace of God, they're still standing, but abuses inflicted on a young girl don't magically disappear. They show up in her story, often unexpectedly.

The husband or fiancé, however, often has no idea what happened, how it has impacted her life, how it will affect their marriage, or what to do about it.

In couples who are dating or engaged, the guy begins to see signs that he cannot understand or explain. For example, it might confound him that his sweetheart can be so attractive, yet think poorly of herself. She's actually shocked that he finds her stunningly beautiful.

Or, she might shut down whenever they argue. She might equate expensive gifts or sex with love. She might have an unreasonable desire for him to exclude other family members, whom she sees as competition for his love.

Other signs include unexpected angry outbursts. In working with couples, I've seen all these signs and many more. But the young and in-love don't heed them. When you're in love with someone, his or her flaws and quirks are easily overlooked. You think, *Over time, they'll go away.*

My point here is not that women come into relationships messed up, but men don't. Many men bring great challenges, too. Father-wounds that have yet to heal, just to name one. Without a doubt, we all come with baggage. But my concern in this book is to challenge men to avoid discarding a woman because she's "not a perfect package" or has issues, especially after he has committed to her in marriage. Sometimes, when a woman's thinking or behavior seems irrational, a man will throw up his hands and leave.

If you're still dating or engaged and you choose not to embrace the weaknesses you see, you're free to leave. But do keep in mind that *whomever* you connect with for lifelong companionship will have her own weaknesses. And you have your issues too. The courageous coverer will look a woman's pain in the eye, love her, cherish her, and nurture her to her full potential in Christ.

Don't Be "Scurred"

The commitment to cover a woman who was damaged as a child or teen takes the courage to endure turbulent relational waters. In this situation, a man is called to embrace his woman, and her past, on the way to the future they envision.

> *The commitment to cover a woman who was damaged as a child or teen takes the courage to endure turbulent relational waters. In this situation, a man is called to embrace his woman, and her past, on the way to the future they envision.*

If you find yourself in such a relationship, you might discover things that anger or confuse you. You might find the lady you love has no idea how to relate to you as a man. She might not know how to respect you, because her father figure was not respectable. She may want to remain independent, rather than depend on you for anything at all. She may have a need to control every facet of home life, including the clothes you wear. You may feel like distancing yourself from her. Don't. The two of you might need to find a wise biblical counselor who specializes in marriage and family dynamics. Don't hesitate to embrace such a resource.

Recently, a couple came to me with marriage problems. They were only a year into the marriage, but he'd already walked out three times.

Each time it was because he was deeply disappointed by her lack of respect for him. Both, by the way, were competitive college athletes. But she grew up as the self-assigned protector of her home, after her father abandoned the family for another woman. She made it her job to lock all the doors at night and to see that her siblings were safe from harm.

If you saw this gentle and godly woman in person, you'd never guess that she could assume such a strong leadership role. But her protective role has been her way of avoiding more pain. That works fine when you're growing up without your dad. It can be a recipe for disaster when you marry a strong, capable man.

This couple's disagreements led to painful and disrespectful words that drove him away from her emotionally and physically. In the beginning, he had no idea that her broken relationship with her dad would affect their marriage so profoundly. Now he does.

She's working on her words now. And now he knows the *worst* thing he can do to a wife who was abandoned is to walk out the door himself. He must be courageous enough to see the pain in her, go through the heated battles, and yet resolve to never leave again.

Take a Good Look

When a man is attracted to a woman, he sees everything but the painful past that has shaped her and made her who she is. But the signs are there. You just have to know what you're looking for. To guys, I always suggest, "Look at her dad's role in the family, and in her life in particular."

I give this advice because we men are usually so enamored with her body or her smile or how she makes us feel that we miss blaring "father factors" in her story.

Men, ask her to share her story, and pay attention. Here are some questions you can ask:

"Did you grow up in a home with both parents or with one?"

"Who was your primary care-giver?"

"Are you adopted?"

"What is your current relationship with your father?"

"Was your dad faithful to your mom?"

"Was your father addicted to drugs or alcohol?"

"Did your mother and father spend a lot of time together—even if they were divorced?"

"Was your father a gambler, a workaholic, or a porn addict?"

"Did your father travel a lot for work?"

"Did he provide for your physical needs—and was he emotionally engaged as well?"

"Did he keep his word to you?"

"Did he ever hit you or your mother? Was he abusive in any way to his family?"

If you want to know about the woman you are (or may be) covering in marriage, the answers to the above questions will tell you what you to expect. You'll get a sense of her needs and how she might relate to you as a man. You'll discover some of her fears or her joys; some of her expectations and some of her resolutions. You might be intimidated if she had an exceptional relationship with her dad. Good. In that case, make sure you develop a good relationship with him too.

Some women have had horrible relationships with their dads, but they may be in the healing process through counseling or a great women's ministry in their church. Celebrate and encourage that with her. Her dad may still be alive and could be a better man now than he was then. Take a look. But whatever you do in this process, do not ignore her relationship with her father. He has affected her life. That cannot be disregarded. If that relationship wasn't good, don't treat her like she's damaged goods and run away. Seek to understand the impact it had on her, and choose to cover her like a real man.

Assure Her, "It's OK."

Some of the things you hear when you talk to your wife or fiancée or someone you (appropriately!) cover are tough to absorb. I find it difficult to hear the hurtful things many teens and adult women have suffered. Whether it was neglect by a father or sexual abuse or verbal abuse by an ex-boyfriend, the stories are gut-wrenching.

But if these stories are hard for you to hear, think about how difficult they are to *tell*! When a woman reveals intimate things about her life, she shouldn't be judged or treated differently after the fact. Don't ask "Why didn't you . . ." questions. If she could have avoided or stopped a tragedy from happening, she would have. So don't make her feel that what she suffered was her fault.

Especially with a wife or fiancée, the most important thing you can offer is the assurance that you love her and that you will be there for her. She'll struggle sometimes, wondering what you think and whether what she shared with you has lowered your opinion of her. She needs assurance that you do not think less of her and that you desire her even more than ever.

If a counselor recommends you go to the appointments with her, then, by all means, make it a priority. If she goes to counseling by herself, drive her if you can. If you can't drive her, call her afterward and pray with her. Let her know you're proud of her for having the guts to step into the healing process. If working through her back-story means putting a wedding on hold or postponing some other major moves--to build a stronger foundation for the relationship-- then do it. But let her know you're not going *anywhere*.

I started coaching a couple a few months ago. They loved each other, but they were having a really hard time progressing in their relationship. They had already set a wedding date, picked out the place, and mailed elaborate invitations. As we began our coaching relationship, it became apparent that they were stuck. What we uncovered together was frightening for both of them. Both of them had been unfaithful for most of their four-year dating relationship. They embarked on a season of truth-telling and told everything to each other. And I mean *everything*. I learned some things that made me wonder if they could have a healthy marriage.

I made one of the scariest coaching recommendations an engaged couple can receive. I challenged them to postpone the wedding for four to six months so that they could build a foundation of trust. I encouraged her to move where his job is, but for him to find an apartment and allow her to move into his home. He agreed to leave for the apartment before midnight each evening. And they committed to no sex until the wedding day. Meanwhile, we began working through a book together to help them prepare for marriage, and we focused on some of their toughest challenges.

During our conversations, this couple revealed to me that she had been molested by her stepfather for years. He gave her expensive gifts to keep her quiet, which explained her feelings that expensive gifts meant she was loved. It also helped explain her strong outbursts of anger and her tendency to shut down when conflict arose in their relationship. She would become defensive if her fiancé questioned her about almost anything. Being wrong made her feel threatened. She had developed so many poor ways of relating. Inside a woman's body was trapped a beautiful little girl who never *had* the opportunity to be a little girl. She's a delightful young woman, and I could see something wonderful trying to come out of the cocoon.

I recommended a marriage and family counselor and that she try to connect with a women's Bible study in her new church. Both of these people have been a joy to coach. They've followed every step of their accountability. She has made amazing progress. Her outlook and demeanor changed in a few short weeks. What's more, her fiancé made up his mind to love her even when he felt like throwing in the towel and moving on. He has chosen to accept her and her entire story. When so many other men would have thrown up their hands and walked away, he has determined to embrace her, for better or for worse.

Chapter 12 Instant Replay

1. "We are attracted to each other's strengths, but we marry one another's weaknesses."—T.D. Jakes

2. Rather than discard a woman who's been damaged, a courageous coverer will look her pain in the eye and love her.

3. If the woman you love was once in a bad relationship, don't treat her like she's damaged goods and run away. Seek to understand the impact it had on her, and choose to cover her like a real man.

CHAPTER 13
Leading By Example:
The Covering Revolution

13

Imagine grade schools where little boys open the doors for little girls and allow them to go first in the cafeteria lines. Imagine churches where boys are taught to be gentlemen and are expected to never put their hands on girls in a violent or threatening way. Can you imagine a nation in which cable TV outlets, radio stations, and YouTube refuse to play songs and videos that belittle and demean young women? Imagine with me a nation where a generation of boys is being raised to deeply respect the opposite sex, never using obscene words to address them.

Call me a dreamer if you like, but I know that nothing great comes about without a dream of something unseen.

As I observe many of our youth, it's clear that they are uncertain how to handle the opposite sex. Boys do hit little girls, call them names, and rush through the doors ahead of them. Unless these boyish behaviors are addressed by men, most boys will not mature when it comes to the treatment of women.

A few days ago, I drove by a handful of teenage boys and girls just after their school day had ended. What I saw made me shudder. One young man had his right hand on one of the girl's throats, with a firm grip. The other kids looked on, laughing. They seemed, frightfully, accustomed to the behavior. It made me wonder what those youth had seen modeled to them, especially the young men.

Boys need strong role models and mentors to instill in them the practices and principles associated with covering. Let's believe God together for a covering revolution in our nation! We can bring it about as men if we begin to teach it and model it to the next generation. But we have to be intentional and persistent. And we have to begin now.

Model With Your Mouth

Words have power. Jesus said it well, "Out of the abundance of the heart the mouth speaks." (Matthew 12:34 NKJV) And the writer of Proverbs 18:21 said, "Death and life are in the power of the tongue." (KJV)

That's why a covering revolution will begin with our language. Cultures are shaped and changed by the conversations people have. Destinies of people, communities, and nations are usually determined by the person with the microphone. Dr. Martin Luther King Jr. forged a new outlook for America through his words. He wasn't the richest man in America. He faced overwhelming political and legal opposition, but he understood the power of words to inspire and to move people.

The conversation in America has shifted dramatically, and we must bring it back to civility, kindness and respect. Sadly, our English language contains more egregious terms for women than any other I know of. It's really unbecoming that men, born of women, would dare to refer to women by terms only fitting for animals. We use terms that objectify women. Too often, we degrade the very women whom we need to help raise our children. And whatever language the men use, the boys will use.

> *The conversation in America has shifted dramatically, and we must bring it back to civility, kindness and respect. Sadly, our English language contains more egregious terms for women than any other I know of.*

Men, it's time to step up our game. It's time we teach our sons and nephews and students and athletes how to speak to women for their good and for the good of society. Whatever happened to "Yes, ma'am"? Whatever happened to the tender reference, "Daughter," when an older man addresses a younger woman. In the African American community, it was once common to call one another "brother" or "sister."

Once there was an era of politeness and decorum in our social address of one another. All females, from the youngest to the oldest, were called "ladies." That decorum fed our highest ideals and reflected some of our best qualities as a nation. We've never been perfect as a nation, but I'd argue we were so much better then.

How did we allow pop artists to commandeer the language and to elevate linguistic hostility toward women to a cultural norm?

It's worse than casual; it's downright crude. Men, I'm challenging us take the language back. Begin by intentionally addressing girls and women as "ladies," as "sisters," and as "daughters." When you hear derogatory language on your television, in the movies, in the workplace, or in your music, turn it off or leave. Don't let the constant refrain deaden your sensitivity to vulgarity. You're better than that. Refuse to allow your sons and daughters to entertain vulgarity on any device under your roof or in your presence. And call the young men around you to something higher--to become a champion for covering someday. Impress on them the vision for a new kind of man in the culture. They'll feel challenged, and they'll appreciate it someday.

For example, the men of Messiah Community Church are setting the standard in our community and building a great covering culture. We always address the women and the girls respectfully and kindly:

"Good morning, sis."

"Hi, young lady, how are you?"

"Yes, ma'am. Thank you for your help."

And the boys are picking up on it and speaking the same language. It can be done.

No More Mediocrity

Revolutions are not born where mediocrity is accepted. Revolutions begin where the current pattern can no longer be tolerated and someone demands change. Revolution comes from the Latin word *revolutio*, which means to turn around. A Covering

Revolution implies the need to turn something around-- namely the lack of covering for girls and women of all ages. If we are going to provide covering, we must reject the spirit of mediocrity among the men in our churches and in our communities. Average, middle-of-the road manhood is unacceptable. No one wins when the men are mediocre. You and I weren't born for mediocrity. We were born to be a great husbands, great fathers, and great tools in God's hand. This is not about popularity. Remember, I know the NFL. You can be popular but contribute little value to people's lives.

Mediocre people don't stand for anything. They have few convictions, apart from the convictions to be comfortable and undisturbed. Revolutionaries, on the other hand, can't get the vision for change out of their minds. They eat, sleep, and breathe a vision. They're passionate for something that matters, something that benefits humanity.

On the other hand, a mediocre man with no passion and no cause greater than himself is a dangerous man. He can't be trusted, because, at every turn, life is about *him*. Mediocre men aren't passionate for their wives' or children's or co-workers' welfare. They're not passionate about making life better for the next generation. They're concerned about what's in it for them *now*.

If we're going to start a Covering Revolution, it will begin with a few men, like you, who refuse to be mediocre in their marriages, in their parenting, and in their care for others. It will begin with a few men, like you, who refuse to stand by idly while our sons and daughters are swallowed up by the culture. It will begin with men willing to sacrifice our personal comforts for the sake of women and children all around us. The revolutionaries among us will insist that the small but significant things be done, *consistently*. We can open the door for ladies. We can walk on the outside of the sidewalk, putting ourselves between the women and the traffic. We can give up our seats on public transportation so that women and girls have a place to sit. Men, we don't have to do the dramatic. We just need to do the little things that speak covering and remind the world that manners still matter.

My friend, I know who I'm writing to. If you've read this far, you're not a mediocre man. You're a man who wants and expects greatness. After all, who picks up a book called *Cover Her* unless he's committed to getting better?

My friend, I celebrate you! You are a revolutionary, and you're part of the Covering Revolution. Together we're about to turn things upside-down. Don't be surprised when the women you know start asking, "What has happened with you? This is awesome! Are there more men like you around?"

Tell them, "Yes, and they are on the way."

On our way to Super Bowl XLVII, the Baltimore Ravens lost three games in a row, to the Pittsburgh Steelers, the Washington Redskins, and the Denver Broncos. Before those losses, we had a record of 9-2. Afterward, it seemed as if a season of promise was falling apart. Injuries to key players like Bernard Pollard, Lardarius Webb, and team leader Ray Lewis were taking their toll. But while the media and football fans outside the Ravens camp assumed the worst, those of us inside the camp were having a different conversation. To a man, everyone believed the 2012-13

Baltimore Ravens were anything but mediocre. We knew this team was made to accomplish something great.

Coach Harbaugh gave everyone his marching orders: "Do the little things better than anyone else, every day. Get better one practice at a time, one meeting at a time, one game at a time."

And the men took his charge to heart. What happened, in spite of hitting a rough patch, is nothing short of amazing. An entire world of onlookers began to quote the Ravens' Ray Lewis (who had quoted the prophet Isaiah): "No weapon formed against us shall prosper." (Isaiah 54:17) Football fans and "haters" alike were inspired by a team that refused to settle for mediocrity. Men, people will follow you and be inspired by you because you have refused the way of mediocrity and chosen the way of a revolutionary.

Mentor a Young Man

The revolution may not be televised, but it must be transferred, somehow. The next generation, like the next runner in a relay, must be handed the baton. Otherwise, what one generation builds will die in the next. And that generation may suffer worse than their ancestors. The apostle Paul told his young protégé Timothy, "And the things you have heard me say in the presence of many witnesses entrust to reliable men who will also be qualified to teach others." (2 Timothy 2:2)

In the Old Testament, Moses was concerned that Israel's miraculous deliverance from bondage in Egypt and the subsequent giving of the Law at Mount Sinai not be lost on the next generation. He commanded the parents to teach God's laws to their children: "In the future, when your son asks you, 'What is the meaning of the stipulations, decrees and laws the Lord our God has commanded you?' tell him: "We were slaves of Pharaoh in Egypt, but the Lord brought us out of Egypt with a mighty hand." (Deuteronomy 6:20-21)

I've spent my entire Christian life looking for hungry young men to whom I could pass on my faith and the wisdom of life experiences. There are few things more rewarding than helping another young man take his life to the next level. There's no shortage of younger men looking for a mentor--someone to guide them and encourage them. And if you're now committed to covering and serious about the revolution, you have something to pass on. And you *must* pass it on. All you have to do is look around your church or community. There are single moms raising boys, college students facing huge life decisions, and young men who respect you from afar for your knowledge or career success. Ask God to lead you to one or two of them to mentor for a season--perhaps a year, two years, or three.

So many young men have never been taught what it means to cover a woman, but they want to learn. It's been amazing to encounter young men who don't know how to ask a girl out on a date. They're uncertain what to do on a date. They're intimidated to speak with a young lady's father. They've never been taught the ropes of decency and how to treat a woman. But they are now in business, because God has positioned and prepared people like you. And you're ready to hand off the baton to them.

Mentoring serves three very important functions. First, it reinforces to the mentor the importance of the things he's passing on. Every time I mentor a leader or a couple, my convictions grow deeper and my passions are rekindled.

Second, mentoring positions you to make an exponential impact. I charge anyone I mentor to pass on to someone else anything they learn from me. So when you mentor, you are literally speaking into the lives of people you may never meet, and who may be in places around the world you'll never visit. It's the way to maximize your influence.

For example, Matt Birk calls his former teammate Jason Whittle "one of my heroes. Jason showed me what a godly man in the NFL looks like. He showed me how the roles of Christian and football player fit together. He showed me that a Christian football player is the farthest thing from soft or weak."

Jason's influence on Matt was multiplied through the many players, such as those on the Ravens, who responded to Matt's leadership. "There aren't that many older guys in the NFL," Birk explains, "so later in my career I found myself in a natural leadership position. And I found that you're automatically looked up to when you walk your talk."

Many of Matt's former teammates, such as Billy Bajema, Michael Oher, and Ben Grubbs, have talked about how much they look up to him and how much his leadership and example have affected them.

This brings us to our third point on mentoring: When you mentor someone, you are literally a part of changing someone's life and family lineage. When you teach covering principles, you will be spreading the revolution and totally changing the way generations of men see their responsibilities to women. What an awesome privilege mentoring is!

If you're unsure where to begin as a mentor, I suggest reading this book together with a young man, chapter by chapter. Agree on a meeting place to discuss a chapter each week until you reach the end. In addition, you can ask him for a list of topics that he'd be interested to learn about from you. Talk to your Bible study leader or your pastor for Scriptures related to each topic, and you can each read them before a meeting. Whether you meet by video-conferencing or in person, a young man who's serious about being mentored will be grateful that you took the time to invest in his life! Let the revolution begin.

Chapter 13 Instant Replay

1. Boys and young men need strong role models and mentors to show them what covering is.

2. Young males need to learn how to speak to women for their good and for the good of society.

3. If we are going to start a Covering Revolution, we must be intentional about it.

4. Mentoring is an awesome privilege that more men should consider.

CHAPTER 14

The Covenant to Cover

14

In biblical times, God used covenants to relate to His people. Covenants were agreements between two parties, either Divine and human or both human. They stipulated how those parties would function in relationship to one another and what the outcomes would be if the covenant agreements were upheld or violated.

In the Old Testament, God related to His people based on His Law. But the sacrificed blood of Jesus Christ brought about a New Covenant, wherein God has agreed to operate toward His people with grace.

The power of covenants, particularly those initiated by God, was that they bound God to His promises and bound the people to live by God's clear terms. God blessed faithful obedience, but promised curses to the rebellious. The people knew exactly what they could expect, because God always keeps his covenant promises.

Covenants are not like our modern contracts, which usually have an "out clause," relieving the agreeing parties from their obligations under certain conditions. Covenants with God were good until broken by God's people or superseded by a better covenant from God. But the intention was always to enrich relationships.

The most well-known covenants in our day include the New Covenant in Christ's blood, which guarantees our eternal cleansing and forgiveness and our ability to be in direct relationship with God. The other is the marriage covenant, which has fallen on tough times. Both of these covenants are designed to promote and encourage relationship fulfillment.

Unfortunately, we don't talk much about covenant agreements today. But covenants still have an important place in our relationships with God and with people. Job even made a covenant with his eyes, establishing a commitment not to look lustfully on a young woman or virgin. (See Job 31:1) Job bound himself to the agreement with his own eyes in order to preserve his sexual purity and integrity. As with all covenants, Job's was an intentional agreement, not entered into lightly, with a desire to further a deep and abiding relationship with God.

More than 22 years ago, my wife and I established a covenant of marriage. We wrote our vows to one another. In them, I promised her that I would never abandon her. I promised her that I'd care for her in sickness and in health. I promised I would forsake all other potential lovers and focus my heart on one woman only. I'm grateful to say that after 22-plus years, our marriage covenant is still intact. We have honored the vows we made to each other. We enjoy a deeply fulfilling life together. I didn't grow up around a lot of strong marriages. I had no idea marriage could be so good!

Let's be intentional about a Covering Covenant to guide us and to ensure that covering is a part of our everyday vocabulary and behavior. Just like wedding vows, we need a reminder of our commitment to cover our wives and daughters--something that says to them, "I'm serious about covering you. You can count on me."

What if every man who read this book had a Covering Covenant? What a powerful and encouraging statement we would make to those we are called to cover, and to the world!

> *My wife and I have honored the vows we made to each other more than 22 years ago. We enjoy a deeply fulfilling life together. I didn't grow up around a lot of strong marriages. I had no idea marriage could be so good!*

Below you'll find a Covering Covenant that you can complete and make your own. Make copies if you need to. Pray first, however, so you don't enter into covenant lightly. Consider which aspects and types of covering resonated the most with you. Maybe you'll want separate covenants for your wife and daughters.

Perhaps you simply want to be proactive and establish some covering commitments, as a single man, just between you and God. However you feel led of God, write your covenant statements and share them wherever appropriate. Most importantly, be a covenant keeper when it comes to covering. There are some ladies depending on you for covering, and God will honor your faithfulness.

Chapter 14 Instant Replay

1. In the Old Testament, the power of covenants, particularly those initiated by God, was that they bound God to His promises and bound the people to live by God's clear terms.

2. Be intentional about covering. Tell the ladies in your life, "I'm serious about covering you. You can count on me."

3. Never enter into a covenant lightly.

4. God will honor your faithfulness to your covenant.

Covenant to Cover

Covenant to Cover

Finally, why not enter into a covenant relationship with the God who wants to cover you? He is the ultimate role model and source of covering for those who will put their trust in Him. In fact, I believe that being under God's covering is foundational to my providing covering for others. I believe that effective covering requires God's power.

Fortunately, all the groundwork for the covenant relationship between you and God has been done. Repentance and faith are all that are needed from you. Tell God where you have messed up. Tell Him you want to bring your life under His covering. The covenant He established is so significant that He sealed it with blood--the blood of His Son, Jesus Christ. That blood is God's guarantee that all our offenses toward Him are settled. Rich relationship and unending covering are the benefits.

So I encourage you: Jump in. Say yes. And look forward to being covered with God's grace all the days of your life.

Covenant to Cover

My Covenant is to Cover You (Name & Relationship)

Because I'm committed to covering you _____,

you can count on me to: _____

_____

Because I'm committed to covering you _____,

you can count on me to: _____

_____

Because I'm committed to covering you _____,

you can count on me to: _____

_____

Because I'm committed to covering you _____,

you can count on me to: _____

_____

Because I'm committed to covering you _____,

you can count on me to: _____

_____

Signed _____

Date _____